MW00948633

TABLE OF CONTENTS

Introduction 1

Fundamental Hadiths on Qiyamah 4

Why Study Signs of Judgment Day..10

Categories of The Signs of Judgment Day 17

Minor Signs of Judgement Day 23

Death of Prophet SAW 25

Infighting in the Muslim Ummah 26

Martyrdom of Umar RA and Uthman RA 29

The Battle of The Camel..34

The Battle of Siffin...37

Safety and Security of Muslims.......................................44

Turk's Conquest of Arabia 46

Conquest of Constantinople 50

Tall Buildings in Arabia 56

Abundance of Wealth in Muslim Ummah............................59

Widespread Evil in The World 61

Zina Becoming the Norm 63

Fahisha Becoming the Norm...67

Proliferation of Intoxications and Music............................70

Empty Mosques 71

Children Being Disrespectful to Parents 74

Proliferation of Shopping Centers....................................76

Widespread Obesity..78

Increase of Earthquakes..81

Ar-Rum as the dominant civilization 82

Prevalence of Kitabah 85

Prevalence of Ignorance 86

The Mahdi 88

Analyzing Cryptic Hadiths 99

Christian Interpretations of Second Coming of Jesus AS 101

Hadiths About Muslims Conquering India 103

Major Signs of Judgment Day 104

Dajjal 106

Saf ibn Sayyad 111

Hadith of Tamim Ad-Dari 123

All Prophets AS Warned About Dajjal 133

Dajjal Will Be One Eyed 136

Kaffir on Dajjal's Forehead 138

Dajjal shall travel the whole world.................................140

Claim of Being God..141

First Appearance of Dajjal 142

Reason People Will Follow Dajjal 144

Control of Shayateen 146

Dajjal Will cause the Sky to Rain 148

Power to Resurrect the Dead...149

Jannah and Jahannam of Dajjal.....................................151

Other Hadiths About Dajjal 154

Young Man 154

Curley Hair...154

No Children 154

Crooked Legs..154

Eastern land 155

Dajjal Will be Ahmar 155

Description of Dajjal...156

Women will follow Dajjal 156

Dajjal Will Not Enter Makkah or Medina 158

Wars between Dajjal and Mahdi............................162

Period of Dajjal's Existence 166

Followers of Antichrist 169

End of Dajjal 174

Return of Bani Israel to the Holy Land 176

Wars in the of End Times 179

Civil War Between Muslims 183

War that 1% Survive..186

War of the One third..193

Malhama at Bilad As-Sham 197

Khilafa in Ard-Al- Muqaddas 199

Re-Conquest of Constantinople 201

Romans with 80 Flags 207

Christian Understanding of Armageddon 212

Ya'juj and Ma'juj 216

Surah Al-Kahf 217

Surah Al-Anbiya...220

Dhul Qarnayn 221

Hadiths about Ya'juj and Ma'juj.........................225

classical Understanding of Ya'juj and Ma'juj...........237

Location of Ya'juj and Ma'juj..............................242

Why Not to Theorize on Predictions.....................247

Answering People Facing Crisis of Faith.................252

Era of Peace 256

Death of Isa AS 258

Wind from Yemen 261

Jahiliya at the End of Times..262

Quran Will be Taken Back 263

Interpretation of Surah Al-Isra 271

Three Zalazil 280

The Dukhan 282

Sun rising from the West 285

The Dabbat..289

The Great Fire 293

Where Everything Began 297

The Trumpet 299

Introduction

When discussing the signs of Judgment Day, we'll go over all of the major and minor signs one after another, in a chronological way. There will be a lot of detail involved. This Book is going to be a detailed review of all important signs of Judgment Day. Also, Insha'Allah, we will definitely go in very different refractions that are typically not discussed. And we will be very forthright when discussing them.

There are major issues we need to discuss. Like Ya'juj and Ma'juj. What do we say about them? Where are these billions of people? Where are they living? We have to be very forthright. How do we talk about these issues?

Dajjal is he alive or dead? What supernatural power does he have? Does this mean that Dajjal is some mystical force? Or is he an actual entity? These are some things, that have various theories around them. And we will be forthright when discussing these theories.

And the signs of Judgment Day, in every tradition, they are cryptic. This is one of the things that we find even in the conservative Christian movement. Even in the Orthodox Jewish movement.

This is the genre of signs of judgment. In every religious tradition, you have these phrases that might be difficult to unpack. One of the wisdoms might be that, you only recognize it after it happens. And Allah knows best.

We will begin with discussing the signs of Judgment Day. We will divide them into a number of categories. We will mention the minor signs and the major signs. The minor signs as well will be divided into two types of categories. Number one specific incidents or one-off, and number two, general trends.

The general trends will be events that the Prophet SAW predicted would change towards the end of times. And he's mentioning how societal changes will occur. What is going to change in culture. What is it going to change in the way people live; and the way people interact with one another.

Now, there are many other trends that are predicted as well. This isn't the complete list. Obviously, there has to be some condensation over the material. Many other things are predicted as well. And there's another entire section of hadiths that are not authentic. What we'll be mentioning in the book will be every hadith that is authentic Insha'Allah. And to cover all bases, we will inform on what Unauthentic hadiths say on that specific subject.

First, we will be narrating Quran and Sunnah. We will be narrating our sources. Then we will pause and go back and see what we can derive from those sources. Because we need to really think deeply about these things. Because there's a lot of material to digest and discuss.

Fundamental Hadiths on Qiyamah

One of the fundamental pillars of our faith and of our theology is belief in judgement day and the signs of judgment day. Now the concept of Judgment Day and the signs of Judgment Day is something that is actually mentioned in the most fundamental hadith of our religion.

That's the hadith of Jibreel AS. The famous hadith of Jibreel AS, when he came and quizzed the Prophet SAW. Jibreel AS asked the Prophet SAW, "What is Islam?"; "What is Iman?"; "What is Ehsan?". One of the questions in that Hadith that Jibreel AS asked him was, "When is the day of judgement?"

And the Prophet SAW said, "I don't know, same as you don't know". Then Jibreel AS said, "Inform me about the signs of Judgment Day".

Now, the very fact that Jibreel AS is asking this question, when the time is limited, and the occasion is auspicious, shows us the gravity of this movement. Only once in the entire Seerah did Jibreel AS come down in public, so that everybody could see him. This never happened before, and never happened again. And every question that Jibreel AS asked was specifically from Allah Subhanahu WA Ta'ala.

So, the very fact that Jibreel AS is coming down and asking these questions, means that there is an importance to these questions and their answers, according to Allah SWT. Remember Jibreel AS does not come down because he wants to. It is because Allah SWT has sent Jibreel AS.

And at the end of the Hadith, the Prophet SAW some asked the Shaba, "Do you know who that was?" The Sahaba replied, "No". Prophet SAW said, "He was Jibreel AS. And he came to teach you your religion". Which means, every single question that was asked was a fundamental question of the religion. Otherwise, it would not have been asked.

Every question that Jibreel AS asked was of the fundamentals and needed to be answered for us to be clear on its concepts in detail, and one of the questions he asked was about the signs of Judgment Day. This indicates that the signs of the Judgment Day are an integral part of our faith. Otherwise, it would not have been asked.

And that is why the genre of writing books about Judgment Day, goes back to the earliest of times. Every major collection of hadith from Sahih Bukhari, Sahih Muslim, Abu Dawood start with this hadith. In fact, many Muhadditheen wrote special books on this subject starting in a similar way.

Of them is as Nu'aym ibn Hammad RA. He wrote a multi-volume book called 'the signs of Judgment Day', which is an entire encyclopedia written in the third century of the Hijra. And from that time onwards, many books have been written.

Our Prophet SAW used to dedicate special classes for the signs of Judgment Day. How do we know? Abu Zaid Al-Ansari RA narrates in Sahih Muslim, and it is very interesting narration. He says, "One day the Prophet SAW prayed Fajr with us. And then he climbed on the Minbar". Which was not his habit, as he didn't climb on the Minbar after Fajr.

And the hadith continues, "He climbed on the Minbar and he gave us a lecture until Salat of Zohar. Then he came down and he prayed the Zohar with us. Then he went up and he spoke until Asr. He came down he prayed Asr with us. Then he went up, and he spoke until Maghrib".

Meaning, Prophet SAW spoke essentially almost non-stop. we can assume there were smaller breaks. But the point is, one full day class was given to the Sahaba from Fajr until Maghrib. What was the topic of that class? Abu Zaid Al-Ansari RA says, "He taught us what would happen until the day of judgement. And the most knowledgeable of us about the Signs of Judgment Day, is the one who had the best Hifz, and memorized the most on that day".

This hadith is in Sahih Muslim, the most authentic book after Sahih Bukhari. So, there was a class that the Prophet SAW system gave from Fajr up until Maghrib about the Signs of Judgment Day.

How else do we know about this? Other Sahabah were present. The famous Sahabi Hudhaifa ibn al-Yaman RA, the one who kept the secret of the Prophet SAW, he said, "One day the Prophet SAW gave us Khutbah in which he didn't forget to mention anything until the day of judgment. He mentioned everything that will happen".

So, Hudhaifa RA is there, and he's putting it in his own words, that one day Prophet SAW gave them a lecture about everything that would happen. It is the same thing that Abu Zaid Al-Ansari RA said. When two people attend the same lecture, they'll narrate the gist, but there'll be slight differences.

So, they first saying the Prophet SAW gave us a Khutbah, a lecture, that he taught them everything until the day of judgement that would happen. And then he, "Whoever knows it, knows it. whoever doesn't, doesn't. Whoever remembers those, remembers. Whoever doesn't, doesn't".

And then he says something interesting. He said, "And sometimes I see something happening in my life, and it reminds me of something that I had forgotten; that the

Prophet SAW said on that day. Just like one of you doesn't see his friend for many months, doesn't think about him; then he sees his friend and he says, where have you been".

Meaning, the person remembers he had an acquaintance. Like, a person has a close circle of friends, then you have you're 100 other acquaintances that you don't really keep in touch. And suppose somebody of that acquaintance goes missing for a week or two. Then you see him in the Masjid and you ask, 'Oh where have you been?'

In that week you didn't remember him, but when you see him you remember him. This is what Hudhaifa RA is saying. That, "Sometimes I see something and I forgot that I had heard about it before. But when I see it happening, I remember that is what the Prophet SAW had said".

And this is why, when Umar Ibn Al-Khattab RA in his Khilafa asked, "Who amongst you knows what the Prophet SAW has said about the end of times?" It was Hudhaifa RA who responded, "Why do you concern yourself with it Ya Amir Al-Momineen? Don't you know that there's a closed door? You're not going to see those signs".

Umar RA said, "Will that door open with a key, or will it be broken?" And Hudhaifa RA said, "It will be smashed.

It will be broken". That was the prediction that Umar RA would die a Shaheed. He wouldn't die a natural death.

But what did Hudhaifa RA say? "Why are you worried Amir Al-Momineen?" Meaning, 'You're not going to see all of those things. That's going to be after your time. You will be gone'. Notice how Hudhaifa RA said to Umar RA, 'You're not going to see the fitna between the Sahaba'.

Now, how did Hudhaifa RA know this? It was of those things that the Prophet SAW mentioned in cryptic language. Because the Prophet SAW didn't say things out literally. But he is speaking in a language that the intelligent Sahaba understood.

So Hudhaifa RA understood roughly in what era what events will take place, and what events from the Prophet SAW's Hadith are going to happen in his life time etc. And therefore, he understood that Umar RA will not live to see any of the Fitna and he will die the death of a Shaheed.

Why Study Signs of Judgment Day

Now, let us begin with why are we studying signs of Judgment Day? What are the benefits of studying this branch of Islamic theology? Realize that Allah Subhanahu WA Ta'ala has mentioned in the Quran that, "The Day of Judgment is very close. Don't think it is far away. It is very close".

Allah Subhana WA Ta'ala mentions that, "People are quizzing you about Judgment Day, and they ask you about Judgment Day". Allah SWT says, "The signs of judgment they have begun already". Meaning, Allah SWT is telling Prophet SAW to tell us that, 'When people ask you when the Judgment Day is going to come, tell them that the precursors, the flags, the warning signs have already begun'.

Allah SWT says in the Quran, "The judgment is closed". Allah SWT says in the Quran that, "The Hisab of mankind is coming closer to closer". Allah SWT says in the Quran, "They think that Judgment Day is far away, but we know that it is very, very close".

And our Prophet SAW, he predicted, and the hadith is in Sahih Muslim; and he put his fingers out; The first two fingers of his hands, and he said that, "Myself and the

Judgment Day have been sent like the distance between these 2 fingers".

So, the Prophet SAW is signifying the closeness of Qiyamah by pointing to the distance between two fingers; which is a small amount. The coming of the Prophet SAW and Judgment Day has very little time between them. So, the coming of the Prophet SAW is the beginning of the signs of Judgment Day. With his coming, with his birth, with his mission and then with his death, this is the beginning of Judgment Day, or the beginning of the signs of the Judgment Day.

And our Prophet SAW said, and the Hadith is in Sahih Muslim, that, "O my Ummah, your example of the time that you have, compared to the times of the Ummah before you, is like that of a person who has prayed Asr, and he's waiting for Maghrib. And that will be Judgment Day".

We are the people that have prayed Asr, and are waiting for Maghrib. Everybody else prayed Fajr, Zuhr, and Asr. The previous Ummahs were way before us. The time slot between Asr and Maghrib is the shortest. We barely pray Asr, and before we know, it's Maghrib time. And the previous Ummahs they are the previous Salawat.

Therefore, the Judgment Day and the signs of Judgment Day are something that make us waking up to the reality of the actual Qiyamah.

In one hadith is Musnad Imam Ahmad, our Prophet SAW said, "I was sent along with the day of judgment. And I just preceded it". Meaning, he is saying, 'It almost beat me'. This is an authentic hadith in Musnad Imam Ahmad. That it is as if Allah SWT sent the both of them together, and the Prophet SAW just beat the day of judgment by a little bit.

So, given the fact that fourteen hundred and forty years have passed since the Prophet SAW said that. And that is a millennium and a half. That is a huge step in human history. All of recorded human history does not go back more than six thousand years.

The earliest actual records that we have of any civilization are Six thousand years old at max. Yes, we have remnants of people seven, eight thousand years old. But there are no proper written histories. We don't know the dynasties.

Of these Six thousand, one thousand four hundred is our own Ummah. So how about the previous Ummahs before? How about the Ummahs before the recording of history? How about the Ummahs that go back to Nuh AS and period before him? How many tens of thousands of years have passed? Only Allah Subhana WA Ta'ala knows.

And now, we have just a little bit of time left. As Allah SWT says in the Quran, "The Judgment Day is like the twinkling of an eye. It's like your eye blinking. Or it is even faster than that". And if you look at how long this world has been here. Billions and billions of years. And how long human beings have been here.

At the very least 50,000 years we Homo sapiens have been here. Then what is 1400 years? It is nothing. And that's why our Prophet SAW said that, "I am the first of the sign. My death is going to be the first of the major signs of Judgment Day". Meaning major in the sense of beginning the signs of Judgment Day.

And Allah Subhana WA Ta'ala reminds us that, "Are they waiting for Judgment Day? Can't they see the signs of Judgment Day have already come?" And Allah SWT mentions that, Isa Ibn Maryam AS is also one of the signs of Judgment Day. It is in Surah Az-Zukhruf verse number 61that, "Isa and the coming of Isa is a flag for Judgment Day". But this ayah is talking about the second coming of Isa AS and not the first coming of Isa AS.

And the Quran also mentions the coming of Ya'juj and Ma'juj. So, all of these are signs that are mentioned in the Quran about Judgment Day. What is the reason?

Why we are studying these signs? There are many reasons.

Of them, the primary reason is that it makes us appreciate the truthfulness of our Prophet SAW. When we see things that he could never have known, things that are impossible to know, when we see that he's predicting the future, and we are living that future; how can our Iman not go up? How can our Iman not be confirmed? How can we not have Yaqeen that this man, he is not a normal human being, in the sense that he is not speaking from his mind. He is speaking from Allah Subhana WA Ta'ala, who is inspiring him.

And when we hear of these predictions, when we see the specific, very interesting predictions; that nobody could have thought of, and he is telling them to us, and we see them before our eyes; then our Iman increases in Allah SWT, in the Quran, and in the Sunnah as well.

Why else are we studying Judgment Day? And the signs of Judgment Day, they are like the symptoms of a disease. When you see the symptoms, you should be concerned. You should take precautions. What happens when your cholesterol level goes up? You start monitoring your food. What happens when your sugar level or when your heart beat Is not normal? You start taking adequate measures to protect yourself.

So, what will be the case, when you realize that Judgment Day is around the corner? That Qiyamah is coming closer and closer. What are you going to do? You will take precautions. You will become more aware. You will feel the need to prepare for Qiyamah.

So, one of the main factors why we are studying signs of Judgment Day is that, it impacts our life. We live better lives. So that we are prepared to meet Allah Subhana wa Ta'ala on the day of judgment. So, it is a wake-up call for us that we realize that the end is near, and we need to prepare ourselves.

And of course. of the reasons that we study the signs of Judgment Day as well is that, Insha'Allah this gives us a sense of comfort. Let us be brutally honest. Wallaahi, we live in depressing times to be honest here. So much is going on that the heart bleeds. What is happening around the world? Where does one begin.

Now you read these Hadiths and you realize a lot of this has actually been predicted. The very fact that it has been predicted, puts things in to perspective. Let me give you an example. If the doctor tells you you're going to go through some sickness before it gets better. When it goes down, it's painful.

But when the doctors told you that it is going to go down, doesn't that knowledge keep you mentally prepared? The doctor told you it is going to be hard for a week. It's going to be difficult. That prediction of the doctor, that forecast, it gives you a sense of peace. That the end will be better.

This is the point. When we study hadiths about Judgment Day, and these hadith they, have a lot of warnings, but they also have some good news with them. They also have some Basharat. So those warnings they're not going to make us depressed. We are mentally prepared. We are psychologically prepared. We are emotionally prepared.

And when we see it happening, when we see those trends, our Iman goes higher. We turn to Allah Subhanahu wa'ta'ala. And we feel a sense of comfort that Insha'Allah Allah SWT will take care of us. Because why do you think our Prophet SAW told us these hadiths? Why did he tell us that my Ummah will be split up?

Not to get us depressed. Not so that we feel down. No. He told us to give us the comfort that we need. To give us the moral support, and the encouragement. He told us so that Insha'Allah Ta'ala when it happens, we are prepared emotionally and mentally for dealing with those signs of Judgment Day.

So, these are some of the reasons why we will study the signs of Judgment Day.

Categories of The Signs of Judgment Day

Now, how do we categorize the signs of Judgment Day? There are so many hadiths. So many verses in the Quran. So many traditions of the Prophet SAW. Over a dozen works have been authored in classical Islam on this topic. By classical, I mean basically the first eight hundred years of the Hijra.

Of the early stage of Islam, Ibn Kathir RA is one of the most comprehensive. When he wrote his book 'Al-Bidaya Wan Nihaya', 'The Beginning and The End', he put an entire volume in the end for signs of Judgment Day. And many authors before him and after him, they wrote special treatises about the signs of Judgment Day.

So, when they're looking at all of this material, when they see all of these a hadith in front of them, they try to categorize them. And categorization is a well-known science. And how you categorize is all relative. We categorize people based upon gender, male or female. We can also categorize based upon work, engineer or doctor. We can categorize based upon ethnicity. For the same group of people, there can be different categories.

Similarly, when it comes to signs of Judgment Day, you have the same set of hadiths that can be categorized in to various groups. How you categorize it, that can be different.

So, one way to categorize, is to categorize it into one of two; either a specific incident, or a general trend. Some predictions can be one incident. Like Muslims shall conquer Constantinople. That's a one off. In another hadith, the Muslims will conquer Rome. That's a one-off incident.

That Dajjal will come; that's a one-off incident. Ya'juj and Ma'juj will be released, that's a one-off incident. The Mahdi will come, that's another incident.

Or you have a trend. Example of a general trend can be that, ignorance will prevail. And one hadith, writing will be common. This is a very interesting prediction. And imagine in a society when the Prophet SAW was sent in Makkah, barely twelve people knew how to read and write.

Most of the Sahaba of early Islam were not literate. Because it wasn't in the culture of the Arabs at the time to be literate. And our Prophet SAW said, "One of the signs of Judgment Day is that the majority of mankind will write". This is a trend. It is not a one-off. You see that one of the signs of Judgment Day is that everybody will be taking drugs and alcohol.

It is one of the signs of Judgment Day is that immorality will prevail. That people will be doing it in public or nudity will be public. This is a trend. It's not a one incident.

So, these are two ways two categorize; a one incident and a trend. And this is something that is very clear now.

Another way to categorize these hadiths, which is the more common way, and it is the one that we will be using Inshallah; that is to divide the science of judgement day into what is called major signs and minor signs. And where do we get this from?

We get it straight from the hadith of the Prophet SAW. There are a number of authentic hadiths of the Prophet SAW, where he explicitly mentioned that there are going to be 10 major signs of Judgment Day. So, by mentioning that ten signs will be major signs, automatically this means that the rest are going to be minor signs. So, the Prophet SAW is the one who brought forward this categorization.

And the hadith is in Sahih Muslim, that our Prophet SAW came across the Sahaba one day. They were sitting in the Masjid. He came, and they were having a heated discussion. So, he said to them, "What are you discussing?" So, they said, "We are talking about when Qiyamah will happen?" They are talking about and making a guess about when Qiyamah will happen.

So, the Prophet SAW said that, "the Qiyamah will not happen until you see its 10 signs". So now, he has said there are 10 signs that are directly linked to Qiyamah. There are 10 signs that are definitely in a different category, and Qiyamah will not happen until you see those 10 signs happening.

Then he mentioned them one by one. And I'm going to quickly list them for now. And by the way, all ten of these are specific. These are not trends. All ten of these are one-off incidents. These are clear-cut signs that something major, catastrophic, and cataclysmic is going to happen. And everybody will recognize this is one of those major signs.

And the order in which the Prophet SAW mentions these events is not according to the chronological order in which these events will take place. Meaning, they don't necessarily have to be in this order.

Number one, he said, "The Dukhan". The Dukhan is a dust, smoke, smog. Number two, the Dajjal. Number three is the Dabbat, the beast. And it is mentioned in the Quran. Number four is the rising of the Sun from the West. The Sun rises in the East and sets in the west. One day it will rise from the West.

Number five, the coming down of Isa Ibn Maryam AS. This is a specific incident and that is not ambiguous at all. It is very clear. Number six, the coming of Ya'juj and Ma'juj. That is also a major sign.

Number seven, eight and nine, are the three earthquakes that will shake the world. It is going to be a major event. This isn't going to be a regional earthquake. These are earthquakes that essentially the world will know that it is an earthquake unlike others. And in one hadith it says that each next one will be bigger than the first one. So, there will be three consecutive earthquakes that are taking place.

And then number 10, he SAW said, "The last of these signs is a blazing fire that will emanate in Yemen and will force the people towards the land of Resurrection". The very last sign of Judgment Day will be the fire, that will force people to gather in one place. And that will be the end of humanity in that one place. Which is going to be in Balad al-Sham.

In another hadith, The Prophet SAW said, "Anytime, one of these ten signs come, expect the other to come immediately after". So, these ten signs are like dominoes. When the first one comes, Khallas, the rest are going to follow very, very quickly. And the first of these ten signs, without a doubt, is the coming of Isa Ibn Maryam AS.

And when Isa AS comes, the rest of these are going to come one by one. And then Qiyamah will take place very shortly after the coming of Isa Ibn Maryam AS.

And the last of the minor signs, links to the first of the major signs. The last of the minor signs is the coming of the Mahdi. And the Mahdi will be alive and will interact with the first of the major signs. And that is Isa Ibn Maryam AS. So, the Mahdi and the Isa AS will coexist at the same time, same place. And will interact with one another. It is literally as if the minor signs are coming to an end, and the major signs are beginning. And then the rest will go from there until Qiyamah.

Minor Signs of Judgement Day

Now, we will be discussing some of the primary minor signs of Judgement day. Now, there is an exhaustive encyclopedic list of minor signs in the greater books of Hadiths, with a lot of detail about various narrations, and how authentic they are.

What we will be seeing here are the more significant of the minor signs that are called from the prior books. So, by no stretch is this list fully comprehensive. And we have one of the most comprehensive books and the most encyclopedic book ever written. It is Kitab un Fitan by the famous scholar of hadith of the 4th century, Nu'aym ibn Hammad.

It has almost around a thousand narrations about the signs of Judgment Day in his book hadiths and he's in the classical timeframe of scholars. He is in the time frame of right after Imam Bukhari RA. So, he's writing every hadith with Isnad to the Prophet SAW. It is a massive compendium that was very recently edited and published. Otherwise, it was missing for many centuries. But they came across and it was recently printed.

This is a massive encyclopedia and that it is not going to be possible to completely narrate them all in the length of this book.

So, let us begin Inshallah by discussing about some of the more significant of these minor signs and we will mostly be using authentic hadiths for this. And we will inform of weak hadith when we reference them.

And we will see which is the position of the vast majority of the scholars of our religion. Including Imam An-Nawawi RA and Ibn Taymiyyah RA and others; who said that weak hadith, that are not 100% authentic, they may be used with a number of conditions.

You must have some conditions attached to them. No classical scholar completely rejected weak hadith. This is actually a modern opinion of the classical Ulema and the medieval Ulema.

So, a Zaeef hadith can only be accepted with a number of conditions. One of them being that, you point out that this hadith is weak. And so, you have a yellow light, to be cautious when discussing that hadith. So, some of these hadiths will be weak, but most of these will not. And when it is, they will be pointed out. Otherwise, the default in these lists is authentic hadiths, Insha'Allah.

Death of Prophet SAW

The first of the minor signs that we have already mentioned, which is the birth of the Prophet SAW; and the Dawah and the message of the Prophet SAW; and the death of our Prophet SAW.

This all together is the first of the signs of Judgment Day. This is where it all begins, and that's why he said, "Myself and judgement day, we come as close as two fingers of your hands".

Notice, he's putting himself as the first sign, because he is the first sign. And in the other hadith, he says, "Allah SWT sent the both of us together, and I just came ahead by a slight moment."

That hadith is in Musnad Imam Ahmed. So, he is the first and the beginning of all of the minor signs of Judgment Day.

Infighting in the Muslim Ummah

Of the minor signs that are mentioned in at least a dozen different hadith, is the prediction that the Sahabah themselves would fight each other. This is in a number of authentic narrations, that the Sahaba themselves would be fighting one another. And that, "Once the sword will be lifted amongst the Muslim, the Ummah would continually be fighting until Judgment Day".

And that's why Hudhaifa RA said to Umar RA, 'What are you worried about? It's not going to happen in your lifetime. it's going to happen after your lifetime". And that's why Uthman RA, when he was surrounded by those evil people, he said, "I'm not going to be the one to open that sword".

That was the famous phrase he said, that he will not be that one to unsheathe the sword. Because whoever is the first to do it, will be responsible for, as it will never be put back in until Judgement day. And he knew this. And we know what happened when those evil people, the Khawarij, did what they did.

They assassinated Uthman RA, and they started all of those trials and tribulations. And once it happened, Subhan Allah, up until our times the Ummah has been divided. So, this is a genre of predictions, that there's going to be infighting amongst the Muslims. And with that they will be divided and they will go to war with one another. And they will shed the blood of one another.

And this is one of those things the Prophet SAW was saddened by. In the famous hadith, which is in Sahih Muslim. He said, "I asked Allah SWT for three things. He gave me two of them. And he did not give me one".

By the way, this hadith is so powerful, that even our Prophet SAW, he does not have Haqq that whatever he says happens. Only Allah SWT can say Kun Faya Kun. Even the Habib SAW, the Mustafa SAW, the Ahmed SAW, the Muhammad SAW; even he cannot demand to Allah SWT. He can ask, and it is up to Allah SWT to grant it or not.

What did Allah SWT didn't give him? The Prophet SAW says, "I asked him to never cause an external enemy to come and eliminate my Ummah, and he gave it to me". So, never will the Ummah be destroyed in its entirety, by an external force. You might have a section destroyed. But the ummah as a whole will never be overcome in such a manner.

And our Prophet SAW said that some Ummahs before us were destroyed by external enemies. So, he made a dua to Allah SWT for the Ummah to be protected, so that external enemies will never eliminate all of them. Allah SWT said, "You have it".

He said, "O Allah, let no disease or plague eliminate my entire Ummah". Because some of the previous Ummahs were eliminated because of viruses and diseases like Black Death etc. And Allah SWT gave it to him. So, never will the Ummah be eliminated because of an internal disease.

Then the third one, he said, "Oh Allah SWT, let my Ummah not fight one another. And Allah SWT did not give me that". And this is in the Quran that, "no one can challenge Allah SWT for what Allah SWT decides. You will be asked why you did that. No one can ask Allah SWT, why did you do something".

And for a wisdom known to Allah SWT, he did not give this to our Nabi SAW. So, this is one genre, the internal fighting of the Ummah.

Martyrdom of Umar RA and Uthman RA

Another prediction of the minor signs of Judgment Day, and this is in at least five hadith in this regard, if not more. He predicted, explicitly, the martyrdom of Umar RA and Uthman RA. And he implied, that Abu Bakr RA would not die as a martyr, but he would die a natural death. And there are many hadiths in this regard.

And again, Hudhaifa RA understood this. This was why he said to Umar RA that he will not die a natural death, and that the door will be broken. How did Hudhaifa RA know? The Prophet SAW did not mention names. But the concept was there.

In the famous hadith reported in Sahih Muslim, that once the Prophet SAW was with Abu Bakr RA, Umar RA, and Uthman RA. They were walking on the mountain of Uhud, and Uhud began to tremble, it began to shake. So, our Prophet SAW he took his foot and he tapped it and he said, "Uhud calm down". Some scholars say it was trembling out of love and respect for all four of them.

Now, from an Islamic perspective, we believe that inanimate objects have consciousness. This is something that's a part of our faith. We believe the walls, the stones, the Sun, the moon; they have a type of consciousness different than our own. I'm not saying they see and hear like us. But they are aware.

And many modern philosophies and many theories of physics and biology also prove that plants etc. have a type of consciousness, which not like ours. And this is proven in so many Ayahs and Hadiths.

Of them is the Ayah of Quran that says, "Nothing is there, except that it praises Allah SWT". The sun praises Allah SWT. The moon praises Allah SWT. These are inanimate objects. How can they praise Allah SWT? Because they have consciousness.

One of the hadiths is that, when the Prophet SAW picked up the stones, the Sahabah said, "We heard the stone say Subhan Allah, when it was in the hand of the Prophet SAW". The hadith is in sahih Muslim.

Then there is a famous Hadith in Buhari, that the Prophet SAW used to give the Khutbah on Minbar, made out of the trunk of a tree. Then he had an elaborate three-step Minbar constructed for him. So, he left that old tree and started giving Khutbah on the new Minbar. Allah SWT then allowed the trunk of the tree of the old Minbar it's expressions to be heard. Not that the expressions were not there. But Allah SWT allowed the Sahabah to hear how the tree felt.

Think about that. The tree was feeling something. If Allah SWT had willed it just like now, the Sahaba would not have heard or noticed it. Just as we cannot hear the Sun, the moon, the trees, the stars. We cannot hear the walls. At that point in time, Allah SWT blessed the Sahabah to hear, to be on the same wavelength of communication, as this trunk tree. So, they heard it in a language that they could understand.

And they said we heard it sobbing. In one narration, like a baby boy. In another narration, like a camel that has been separated from its mother. This was the expression that Allah SWT gave to the ears of the Sahabah, so that they could understand how the tree felt.

So, what did the Prophet SAW do? He interrupted the Khutbah, and he came down and he hugged the tree. Even inanimate objects feel the love. He hugged the tree and he patted it to calm it down.

Then he ordered that the tree be dug out and be buried where the prophet SAW stood. To this day, it is buried under the Minbar that the Prophet SAW used. So inanimate objects have consciousness of what is going on in their own way.

So, Allah SWT allowed Uhud to express how it felt. And the Prophet SAW said, "Calm down Uhud, you only have a Nabi, a Sadiq and two Shaheeds on you". Notice, he predicted here. Everybody understands that Nabi is

Prophet SAW, Abu Bakr RA is the Siddiq, and then Umar RA and Uthman RA they both die as Shaheeds.

Also, in the famous narration as well, that Abu Musa Al-Ashari RA was with the Prophet SAW, and he followed him. The Prophet SAW went into the garden of one of the Ansar. The Prophet SAW knew that the Ansari would not mind him coming in there. So, he walked in, and he sat down in contemplation.

Abu Musa Al-Ashari RA said, "I will volunteer to be the doorman of the Prophet SAW and the guard of the Prophet SAW. I don't want anybody to disturb him when he's in his Ibadah". So, he went outside and he stood outside of the garden.

When he went outside, Abu Bakr RA came and asked, "Where is the Prophet SAW?" Abu Musa RA replied, "He's inside". Abu Bakr RA Asked, "Can I go inside?" Abu Musa RA said, "Let me ask the Prophet SAW". Abu Musa RA went inside asked the prophet SAW, "O Messenger of Allah SAW, Abu Bakr RA is at the door. Can he come in?"

The Prophet SAW said, "Yes, tell him to come in, and tell him that he shall enter Jannah". Then Umar RA came and the same thing happened. But When Uthman RA came, the same thing happened, but Prophet SAW said, "After a calamity that will befall him. After a Musibah that he will be tested with. Then he will enter Jannah".

So, the Fitan began in time of Uthman RA. Even the assassination of Umar RA was by one deranged lunatic. It wasn't a conspiracy. As for Uthman RA, it was a mob of people that broke up, out of the unity of the Ummah.

And in the famous Hadith in Sahih Muslim, our Prophet SAW said to Uthman RA, "O Uthman, Allah SWT will give you a shirt to wear, and others will come wanting to snatch that shirt away from you. But do not give them that shirt until Allah himself takes it away".

This is a prediction. Now did Uthman RA understood this when it was said? Maybe he did. Maybe he didn't. But he clearly understood it in his Khilafa. This is the point of predictions of Judgment Day, that they are cryptic. Why is this shirt being mentioned? Because the shirt was representing the Khilafa in the context of the hadith. And that is one of the reasons he did not give up the Khilafa. and he died as Shaheed.

So, the Sahabah understood that in Uthman RA's time the door will be opened, and that's when the issues will take place. So, this is the genre of predicting Abu Bakr RA, Umar RA, and Uthman RA's deaths.

The Battle of The Camel

Another prediction, is the prediction of the battle of the camel. And the battle of the camel was the most tragic battles of early Islam, of the time of the Sahaba. There is no exception. It was the most heart-wrenching battle. Because that's the Battle in which on one side you have Aisha RA, Talha RA and Zubair RA. And on the other side you have Ali Ibn Talib RA and many of the other Sahaba.

And this is why, when Imam Ahmed ibn Hunbal RA was asked, "What happened during that time? Which side should we have taken?" Imam Ibn Hunbal RA died in 240 hijra. Two hundred years after the Battle of the camel. It is called the Battle of the camel because Aisha RA was on a camel that had a mini tent.

Our mothers, they were not allowed to be seen at all. Unlike other ladies, that can be seen in Hijab, our mothers, the wives of the Prophet SAW, they cannot even be seen in hijab. They have to be in a mini tent. No one can even see the outer shape of our mothers. This is a special commandment only for them.

So, when she was on the camel, everybody could see the camel bobbing up and down in the middle of the battle, and usually you don't see a woman's tent in the middle of the battlefield, that's why it's called the Battle of the camel.

Imam Ahmed RA was asked about that battle, and he said, "That was a battle Allah SWT saved our swords from having to have blood. So why don't we save our tongues from having to have sides".

Meaning, that was a battle, Alhamdulillah, we didn't have to pick our swords. 'We weren't alive back then. I wasn't forced to choose sides. So then why are you dragging my tongue in and making me force to take sides. Let me be quiet'.

And this by the way, is pure Sunni theology. We stay quiet about what happened between the Sahaba, and we don't discuss it in a lot of detail. We don't bring it up. Because what happens with this kind of discussion? The heart becomes hard, and no benefit happens.

There were people who were righteous. They had a misunderstanding and what happened, happened. We don't dwell on the past. But our Prophet SAW predicted the battle of the Camel.

Hadith is in Musnad of Imam Hakim. And in fact, there are three other hadiths. One of them in Tabarani. And it is an authentic hadith. Now, this Hadid is very mysterious. The first time I read it, I couldn't believe this is so explicit.

So, in this hadith, Aisha RA and Ali RA are sitting in the same room as the Prophet SAW. And the Prophet SAW says to Ali RA, "Oh Ali, what will you do when there will be an issue between you and her? What will you do on that time, when there's going to be some issue?"

So, Ali RA being puzzled, said, "Ya Rasool Allah, Me? How? I will be not be the better of the two". Meaning, Ali RA is saying, 'No that's not going to happen. I'm not going to do that". So, the Prophet SAW said that, "When it does happen, then return her from where she came from safely".

And that is why Ali RA, after the Battle of the camel, he sent his own daughters and he sent the noble ladies of Kufa, as bodyguards of Aisha RA. Meaning, the internal bodyguard. Then you have the external convoy, obviously. He sent the internal bodyguards so that nobody should interact with the women.

He sent his own daughters, and he sent the noble ladies of Kufa, all the way back to Medina to return Ayesha RA to Medina. And then he brought the ladies back. And he left Ayesha RA there. Why? Because the Prophet SAW asked him to do so. And he did exactly as he was commanded.

The Battle of Siffin

The Prophet SAW also predicted the Battle of Siffin. And Siffin was another tragedy. In some ways, it was the worst tragedy than battle of Camel. Both were tragedies. Battle of Camel was the tragedy because you had Ashra Mubashra on both sides. That's painful.

And, by the way one of the benefits of the Battle of Camel and Siffin; and Subhan Allah is so beautiful, because even in problems there is good. Even in some negatives and evils, there is khair that you can derive. One of the khair that we derive is that, righteous people sometimes have arguments.

Good people can disagree with each other. People of Jannah cannot get along in this world sometimes. That's a benefit for us to know that it's possible. It's possible that sometimes you get into an argument and you're both good people. Sometimes people are tested. And righteous people were tested. So much so that they went to war with one another. And yet, they're both the people of Jannah. Subhan Allah, this is this is a lesson.

Now, the Prophet SAW predicted the Battle of Siffin as well. How did he predict the Battle of Siffin? The hadith is in Sahih Bukhari and Sahih Muslim. It is the most authentic hadith imaginable. It's a famous hadith, that the Prophet SAW was on the Minbar, and he's giving the Khutbah. And his grandson, Hassan RA, who was three years old at this time, he comes in. He was wearing a red shirt.

In those days they didn't have much money. So, they would put clothes on their kids that was longer than what they needed, because they could then grow up in those clothes, and those clothes could be used for some time. So, he was wearing a shirt that went below to the floor. Hassan RA, he came out of the house of Fatima RA.

You know how little toddlers are. He sees his grandfather on the Minbar, so he rushes forward, and he tripped on his own shirt. He fell and hit his head, and he began crying in the middle of the Masjid.

Now, the Sahaba are told to listen and be respectful of the Khutbah. Now, who's going to stand up? I mean what are you going to do? On the one hand, the authentic hadith says that, "Don't do anything when the Imam is giving the Khutbah. You here and you obey". On the other hand, Hassan RA is himself crying. What to do?

The Sahaba just stood there frozen. So, the Prophet SAW himself, he came down, and he stopped the Khutbah. He walked between the Sahaba, and he picked up Hassan RA. He calmed him down, and walked back up, and he said that, "I was not able to contain my anxiety when my son was crying". He called him his son.

And every parent knows this that when your child is crying, your concentration is out. Those who have children understand that they can recognize their own child's cry from amongst a thousand sounds. That's why Allah SWT says in the Quran about the Yahood, "They recognize their own children".

Now, The Prophet SAW kissed Hassan RA on the Minbar, and he lifted him up. And he said, "This son of mine is a leader". He called him a son, even though he's a grandson. This is an honor for Hasan RA. Word used in this Hadith is Syed, which means leader.

Then Prophet SAW continued, "And the time will come, when he shall be the cause of reconciling between two large groups of Muslims". Now this hadith is so profound. The Prophet SAW did not criticize either side. And we know what happened between Muawiyah RA and Ali RA. They were fighting constantly. At the death of Ali RA, Hassan RA took charge for a few months.

Muawiyah RA decided to have one more attack, and Hassan RA said, "Enough is enough. You keep the Khilafa". And then he withdrew. And because of that, the Ummah united. And this is the true leader. Not the one who sits on the Chair. But the one who unites the Ummah was called the leader.

Not the figurehead. We respect him. He is a Sahabi. But you cannot compare him with Hassan RA. There is no comparison. The real leader in the metaphorical sense, not in the political sense. Politically, yes, the leader were the Umayyads. But the real leader was the one who stepped back and said, "Enough bloodshed. Let us be one".

Also, the prediction is given as well, in the famous hadith in Sahih Muslim, that Ali RA was fighting the Khawarij. So, Ali RA fought multiple wars. He fought in the Battle of Camel. This is predicted. He fought in Battle of Siffin. This is predicted. He also fought the Khawarij. And the Khawarij are the first sect to break away from the Ummah.

They are first fanatic group to break away. And they consider themselves holier and better than everybody else. And he fought the Khawarij and he won. Then Ali RA said, "Go find somebody who has a deformity of the hand among the dead of Khawarij". And he described in vivid detail, what the deformity is. That there's going to be a black spot.

So, they went once and couldn't find it. Ali RA asked them to search the second time. They went for a second time and they scoured every dead body before they buried it. And they didn't find it. They said, "We looked at every dead body, we didn't find this sign". Ali RA said, "Go for a third time, for Wallaahi, I know what I heard and neither was the person who said this to me was a liar. Nor was I lied to".

In other words, 'the one who said it, spoke the truth and I know what I heard'. So now he got angry, and said 'go find this man'. So, they went, and they found that there were two people who were actually covering a third body. And because of that they hadn't found the third body. So, when they pulled and they found that, that man with the same deformity.

And Ali RA when he saw the body, he said, "Allahu Akbar I know I heard the truth. The Prophet SAW told me that I would fight a group of people and their leader will have a deformity". And the group of people was described as Khawarij and their leader was the person as described to him by Prophet SAW.

This hadith is in Muslim. Imagine how specific of a narration it is, where Ali RA he knows he has to fight this fringe group. And he knows that this is a wrong group. And that their leader is going to have this deformity. This is a prediction. It is one of the signs of Judgment Day.

There's one more hadith in sahih Muslim and Sahih Bukhari. The Hadith states that the Prophet SAW said, "Qiyamah will not come, until a large war takes place between two groups of Muslims who have the same call, and yet they're still having a major war". Now, this hadith is cryptic.

But almost by unanimous consensus, our scholars have understood this to be the Battle of Siffin, or the Battle of Camel, or both. Because it was the only point in time where in reality, theologically, methodologically and religiously, both sides were on par with one another.

In almost every battle after this, generally speaking, it is very different. But in that timeframe, there were no theological differences between these two camps. They didn't differ about Salah, Zakat, Hajj, and Aqidah. It is authentically mentioned that during the battles of Siffin, at the night time, sometimes the two warrior camps would pray together under the same Imam. Because there's no difference in Aqidah.

And once, a person came to Ali RA and said, "Is Muawiyah a Kafir?" And Ali RA replied, "A'uzu Billah, Muawiyah, how can he be a kafir? He ran away from Kufr". So, he said to Ali RA, "Then why are you fighting him?" So, Ali RA said, "I pray in my dua to Allah SWT that me and Muawiyah are like the ones on whom Allah SWT said in the Quran, 'we have removed the animosity between them and they are now brothers in Jannah facing one another'".

Notice, they're fighting one another in the day. But at night, they are making this dua for one another. So, the point being that, the Prophet SAW is saying that two massive groups will fight and they have the same call. It happened during the time of the Sahaba.

Now, in light of the Sahabah fighting, realize that when the Sahabah fought, they were actually three camps. There was the group of Ali RA, and there was the group of Muawiyah RA and then there was a small third category, that refused to take part.

Sahabah like Abdullah Ibn Abbas RA, and Abdullah Ibn Umar RA, they did not participate in either side. And somebody came to Ibn Abbas RA and asked, "Are you in the camp of Ali, or in the camp of Muawiyah?" Ibn abbas RA said, "I am in the camp of Muhammed SAW".

Safety and Security of Muslims

One other prediction, that was truly very strange. And this prediction is one of those, that increases our Iman that our Prophet SAW is speaking from Allah SWT. Hadith is in Sahih Bukhari.

When Ammar ibn Yasir RA was almost tortured to death; when his father Yasir ibn Amir RA, and his mother Sumayyah RA were massacred; when Bilal RA was being dragged through the streets, and his flesh was being used with hot combs; Some of the Sahaba came to the Prophet SAW and complained.

They said, "Ya Rasool Allah, for how long will this happen?" And the Prophet SAW was sitting in the shade of the Kaaba after salat of Zuhr. And the Sahaba are around him. The Prophet SAW said, "How quickly and hastily you lose hope? For Wallaahi, it's only a matter of time when a lady will come from Sanaa to Hadhramaut with her flock of sheep. Fearing none except Allah Subhana wa Ta'ala, and then the wolf attacking her sheep".

Now this is a very strange and yet explicit hadith. He is telling them that in their own lifetime, there will be such a high level of security and safety for the Muslims. Now in those days, there was no central government. Ladies did not travel on their own for their own safety. Especially between two cities.

But the Prophet SAW said that It's only a matter of time, where a new government will arise, that will give so much security and safety, that the furthest nether regions of this land can be traveled without any fear. He mentions two cities far, far away to signify how powerful that new government is going to be. That it shall bring peace and security to the nether regions.

The Sahabah are worried about being physically beaten to death, because they are a Muslim, and the Prophet SAW is telling them a time will come when there will be so much security, that no one will fear the robber and the thief. And as we know, in the time of the Sahaba this happened, and it was manifested many, many times.

This is a prediction that no one could have ever made. When the Sahaba are being cut to pieces, and our Prophet SAW is saying, "We shall be safe, just be patient". Not even one generation, and that is exactly what happened. In their own lifetimes, the Sahabah saw the coming of this peace.

Turk's Conquest of Arabia

Now we move on to the next of the minor signs that have been predicted in the authentic hadith of the Prophet SAW. Of the minor signs, that clearly show the truth of our Prophet SAW; because no one could ever have predicted this. It is the rise of a race that was considered to be a backward race.

This is the race of the Atraaks or the Turks. Our Prophet SAW prophesized that this race would become dominant, and that they would conquer the Arabs. Now who are the Atraaks or the Turks?

The Atraaks are a group of races. It is not just one race within the Turks. Just like how there are many sub-races of Arabs. It's one of the categories of human races. The Atraaks are a group of races who originate essentially from Mongolia and the caucus mountains. They originate from that region.

They are the cousins of the Mongolians. They have a common ancestor between them. And that is why the Turkish language and the Mongolian language, they share many similarities.

Now, contrary to popular misunderstanding, the modern Atraaks, the people of Turkey, are not from that land of Turkey. They are from far more East than that. They are from a land that is called Turkmenistan. That is the land of the Atraaks. The Atraaks came from there and they eventually conquered, what is now the modern day Turkey. And it was called Turkey, because the Atraaks came there.

Before the Atraaks came there, it wasn't called Turkey. That's not the name of that land. It was called Anatolia. The name Turkey, the country Turkey, is after the race of the Atraaks that eventually conquered that region.

Originally, the Atraaks were a far away from the Arabs. The Arabs never interacted with them, by and large. The Arabs hardly interacted with any race other than the Sassanids and the Byzantine Empire.

For our Prophet SAW, in Medina, to predict that, that far away race is going to rise up and eventually dominate Arabs was next to impossible. What is the Ottoman Empire, other than Turkish? This is one of the most miraculous predictions. And these hadith were compiled centuries before the rise of the Ottoman Empire. The Turks rose up 500 years ago, that's it.

And there are many other hadiths on this prediction. Many of these are in Sahih Muslim. The most famous amongst them is where the Prophet SAW used alliteration. Alliteration means things that sound the same, and they have a level of eloquence.

Prophet SAW said, "Leave the Turks as long as they leave you alone. Don't fight the Turks. Because when you will fight them, you will lose and they will win over you". And that is exactly what happened.

Now, some Scholars have said that this could also be a prediction of the Mongol Empire. Because the Mongolians and the Turks go back to the same heritage. So, a thousand years ago, it would not be incorrect to call the Mongols and it would not be incorrect to call Genghis Khan a Turk. Even though in modern times they're two separate ethnicities.

However, other scholars have said that the prediction of Turks here is the Muslim Turks. So, eventually this group of people came, and amongst them were the Seljuks. within the Turkish race. There were many famous dynasties amongst the Turks. The most famous of the earliest dynasties was Seljuk dynasty.

Alp Arslan was the one who came to power, and he was the first of the Turkish people to basically get a base in the lands of Islam. And they converted to Islam. The Seljuk Empire is not the same as the Ottoman Empire. They are both Turkish, but the two of them biologically are different.

So, the first Turkish Empire was the Seljuk Empire. They were magnificent. They came, they conquered and then they dissolved. Then another group came, that was the Ottomans. That was the rise of the Usman tribe of the Turks. Ottomans are the children of Usman.

This is the prediction that our Prophet SAW made that this empire and this group would become the dominant force in the region. And that is exactly what happened. That when the Turks came, they eventually took over the Muslim lands.

So, in the early part of the 16th century they requested from the final remnants of the Abbasid Empire, to hand over the Khilafa to them. And they then acquired the Khilafa. And from around 1,500 up until 1927, Ottoman Empire was the Caliphate of Muslim lands. And it was the only Empire that claimed to be the Khalifa.

There were no non-Arab Khalifa before this point. The Seljuks never claimed to be Khalifa. The Seljuks were a rural dynasty.

Conquest of Constantinople

Another prediction also related to the Ottoman Empire is just as unfathomable. And that is the conquest of the single greatest city in the history of the medieval world. And that is Constantinople. Constantinople, for a thousand years was the bastion of Western civilization.

What will make us understand, what Constantinople was? We hardly study history. We have no idea what Constantinople was. Constantinople for over a thousand years, was the capital of the Roman Empire. Constantine himself named it after him.

Constantine the great established the city as his capital. The city itself existed even before then. And for a thousand and three hundred years, it remained the capital of the greatest empire known to man, up until that point in time. And that was the great Roman Empire.

Europe was nothing at the time. Europe was a backward land. Europe was barbarians at the time. Even Christianity had not spread in Europe. Back then Constantinople was the center of Christendom and of the Holy Roman Empire.

And the Prophet SAW predicted that the Muslims would one day conquer Constantinople. Again, an amazing prediction. How can a small group of persecuted people in Makkah, dream of conquering Constantinople? But the Prophet Saw predicted that.

Now because of this, the Sahaba had it in their minds that they wanted to conquer Constantinople. And in fact, the first Sahabi to launch a campaign to try to conquer Constantinople was none other than Muawiya RA. When he was barely in his early 20s, he managed to come very close to conquering Constantinople via the Navy fleet.

They landed in Cyprus, and then they landed on the banks of the Bosporus, and then they attempted to conquer the city. But it was way too powerful. They laid siege, but they could not do it. It was simply too powerful for them. And the famous companion Abu Ayub Al-Ansari RA, he died outside of the walls of Constantinople.

The famous companion, the one with whom the Prophet SAW lived, in his house, when he entered Medina. The point being that the Sahaba attempted to conquer Constantinople, and their eyes were on the prize. Many Ulema and historians have said that, Tariq Ibn Ziad RA, his main intention for going to Andalus was to make his way to Constantinople by land.

He knew that by sea, conquest would not be possible, because reinforcements would take time etc. He wanted to conquer land by land, until he goes from

North Africa to Andalus, all the way to Constantinople. And Allah SWT knows best.

The point is, many people wanted to conquer Constantinople, but it only happened in 1453 by Sultan Muhammad Al-Fatih. The conquest of Constantinople changed the course of human history. It marked the end of one era, and the beginning of another.

Literally, amongst the ten most famous incidents in all of human history, the conquest of Constantinople will be in the top five. It's that big of a deal that the Muslims finally conquered Constantinople.

The hadith is in Sahih Muslim, that Abdullah ibn Amr Al-A's RA was asked by a Tabi'un that, "Which one will we conquer first? Constantinople or Rome?" They had heard that Rome was there, but Rome was not to the power and the level of Constantinople. It was far number two.

So, Abdullah ibn Amr Al-A's RA said, "Bring me my book". Because he would write hadiths of the Prophet SAW. So, they opened up his book and he looked it up, and he wanted to refresh his memory. And he said, "No, the Prophet SAW predicted that we would conquer Constantinople before Rome".

Now, there is a cryptic prediction about Constantinople that makes it difficult to understand. There are some hadiths that seem to mention that the Mahdi will conquer Jerusalem and also Constantinople. And that is somewhat problematic, because Constantinople has already been conquered. And the Mahdi was not there.

The explicit, authentic hadith in Sahih Muslim, tells us the mechanism via which Constantinople will be conquered. And that is that the Muslims will lay siege for a long time. And they will fall short of supplies. The morale will be going down. Until finally, they will say, "Let us do a Zikar of Allah SWT loudly, and we will conquer Constantinople by way of Zikar".

So, they will began chanting the tasbih, and takbir and eventually the walls of the city will begin to shake and the walls will collapse, because of the Zikr of the Muslims. Now that did not happen in 1453. in 1453 it was an all-out siege.

And one of the reasons the Ottomans could then demand from the Abbasids, to hand over the Khilafa was that; the Abbasids had gone weak because of the Mongol invasion. They had to flee to the Mumluk Egypt. The Ottomans after they conquered Constantinople, they then felt confident enough to call Abbasids as no longer qualified to be the Khalifa.

So, there was a ceremony in which the last of the Abbasids symbolically handed his cloak and his turban to the first of the Ottoman Khalifa. That ceremony actually took place. The Turks didn't feel confident enough to do this until they had the city of Constantinople on silver platter. And of course, they changed of the city from Constantinople to Istanbul.

So how do we understand that hadith? In another hadith, we learn that Constantinople be conquered by seventy thousand children of Ishaq AS. The children of Isaac AS will help conquer Constantinople. How do we understand this? Allah knows best. But it appears that this is talking about another conquest towards the end of times.

It appears that a time will come, where that land will no longer be considered a part of the lands of Islam. That's not the case right now. But something might happen that those lands will no longer be considered the lands of Islam. So once again, there will have to be a reconquest.

Who are the children of Ishaq AS? The Arabs in the time of the Prophet SAW, would call the Romans as the children of Ishaq AS. And this hadith predicts that there will be many Western people that will take part in reconquest of Constantinople.

Because Rome is the western land, that will convert to Islam. And they will be on the side of the Mahdi. And they will be fighting on the side of the truth. And they will then be reconquering Constantinople from whoever else has it at that point in time.

They will use the Zikr of Allah as a weapon, and there will not be violence. There will not be bloodshed. They will simply say Allahu Akbar, Allahu Akbar, Allahu Akbar; and the Zikr will go louder and louder, until as a miracle from Allah SWT the walls of the city will collapse. And they will simply walk in and conquer the city without any bloodshed.

This is something that didn't happen in 1453. So clearly, therefore, there will be another conquering of Constantinople towards the end of times. and Allah SWT knows best.

Tall Buildings in Arabia

Another prediction, and this could be a trend, and it could be a specific incident; Allah knows best. But we are all aware of one of the most amazing predictions that we now see in front of us in our own lifetime. And that is the prediction that, in the Arabian Peninsula, there shall be higher and higher buildings.

In the Arabian Peninsula, there shall be skyscrapers. This is something that, no one could have ever imagined. We need to understand that when Islam came to Arabia, the Arabian people were of the most backward in the world. They did not even have government. They were tribal people.

The basic sign of civilization is government. They didn't have a government. They didn't have a codified language. They did not have a script. The script was developed after Islam. They there was not to single library in all of Arabia. There was no three-story structure. It didn't exist. They couldn't build tall buildings.

That's why, even when they needed any type of technology, they will bring it from outside. Because they're not technologically advanced. They would import their swords from India. They would get their armor from Byzantine. They would import their cloths from Yemen. The Arabs did not have that level of civilization that other lands had.

So, for the Prophet SAW to predict that Arabia and the Arab lands would have the tallest buildings, is once again surreal. How could that happen? And not just that, but people who were only until yesterday dirt-poor, would be competing with one another, to see who is going to build a taller building.

I don't need to go into explicit detail. Wallaahi, this is self-evident. All these rich families that control that part of the world, their own rulers were born in poverty. Listen to the interviews of the senior Princes. Those that are still alive they tell us that when their own fathers came to power, back in the 1920s and 1930s, they weren't rich.

There was no oil back then. These same Princes mentioned, that they didn't have running water. That they didn't have shoes and slippers. That they would run around in the sand. And what did our Prophet SAW say? That, "You will find barefoot Shepherds".

Their ancestors were shepherds. They were barefoot. And now that they are the multi-billionaires; and what do they do? What is their pastime? What is their hobby?

In the year 2000 Al Faisaliyah Center opens up. In 2010 Burj Khalifa opens up. Each one of these Princes wants to show that I have the bigger building. And Burj Khalifa is two and a half times taller than the Empire State Building. Imagine that! And now the other prince of Arabia is building something that is even taller than Burj Khalifa. It's as if, Mashallah, there Iman is so strong, that they want to prove that the Prophet SAW was correct and therefore. They are doing exactly what he said.

The point being that, it is self-evident in our times. We are seeing this farse enacted in front of our eyes. Who could have ever imagined that some of the tallest top ten buildings in the world will be from that region?

Who built them? Shepherds that were born barefoot, and poor. Now, each one is competing with the other to see who is going to build the tallest building. So, these are all specific incidents that have been predicted by our Prophet SAW.

Abundance of Wealth in Muslim Ummah

Now we will move on to the next section of our predictions, and that is general trends. The general trends that the Prophet SAW predicted would change towards the end of times. And he's mentioning how societal changes will occur. What is going to change in culture. What is it going to change in the way people live, and the way people interact with each another.

Of the trends predicted by our Prophet SAW is that, he explicitly predicted that the problem of this Ummah would be an excess of wealth, a surplus of wealth. Not a lack of wealth. Generally speaking, the Ummah would have plenty of wealth. The hadith is in Tirmidhi.

Prophet SAW said, "Every Ummah is tested with one fitna. And the fitna that Allah SWT will test my Ummah with, is money".

Another Hadith is in Sahih Bukhari; that one-day money came from Bahrain and the Prophet SAW was going to distribute it at Fajr time. So, he prayed Fajr, and he saw the Masjid packed like it was Jumma. And he said, "It looks like you have heard that the money has arrived". They said, "Yes".

He said, "I give you glad tidings. Don't worry, you will get your money. But Wallaahi, I am not worried that you will be poor after I die. I am worried that this world will open its treasures to you, and you will compete with one another to see who has the most treasure. And in that competing, you will destroy yourselves; like the nations before you destroyed themselves".

So, the Prophet SAW when there was extreme poverty; When many Sahaba did not even have two pieces of cloth; When in the Medani phase, Ayesha RA says that, "Prophet SAW himself never ate to his full twice"; Six weeks would go by, and Ayesha RA says that they wouldn't light a fire, because they didn't have meat to cook; In that phase, the Prophet SAW predicted that, "My Ummah will be a rich Ummah".

And we have wealth today. Even the lands that are deemed to be poor, their natural resources are of the wealthiest. Even, for example, Afghanistan that has a low GDP, the natural resources in terms of minerals are extensive. The world is salivating over it, because of what it has.

So, the Muslim Ummah is blessed with wealth. Mismanagement and greed are what has destroyed it. But we are a wealthy nation overall. And Alhamdulillah, by and large, in many countries the Muslims are living good lives. Including the ones here in the western lands as well. So, our Prophet SAW predicted this.

Widespread Evil in The World

The Prophet SAW also predicted that evil would be spread across the world. And this indicates many things. For example, he predicted that people will stop trusting one another. That there will be the loss of Amana and trust. He said, "When people stop trusting one another, wait for Judgment Day, as it will be around the corner".

He also predicted the rise of corrupt and evil rulers. He said, "When people who are not worthy, become leaders, wait for Judgment Day. When the worst become the leaders, wait for Judgment Day".

He also predicted that there would be plenty of bloodshed and fighting. He predicted that the Ummah would fight at a time when no two Muslims, who had ever drawn swords against one another, would be killing one another. Imagine that never in the whole Seerah did two Muslims draw blood as a civil war.

In the time of the Prophet SAW this never happened. The two Muslim camps, that later on they went in to fight each other, if you read about it in detail, you will see that it was the Munafiqun that were instigating it.

And the Prophet SAW predicted that the Ummah would continually fight amongst itself until Judgment Day. He said, "Once the sword is unsheathed, it will never be put back in. And the Ummah will constantly fight until Judgment Day".

He also predicted that, not only the Ummah, but overall killing and bloodshed and wars would be increased in the world. And he predicted that people would kill one another for no reason, whatsoever. And this was an unknown phenomenon, that the mass shootings that are common in this land. But we have grown up in this environment and we are accustomed to them.

Every few days we wake up, and some crazed lunatic has killed people for absolutely no reason. We are accustomed to it. We need to understand that this phenomenon does not take place anywhere else in the world, other than this land.

Even this is a recent phenomenon. It is unknown in human history, that people just go on a mass killing for no reason. And our Prophet SAW said, "The judgement day will not come, until the killer and the one killed will not know, why each one did it to the other. Neither will the killer have the motive. Nor the one killed will know the reason for his killing".

This senseless killing without purpose was predicted by our Prophet SAW. And the Hadith is in Bukhari.

Zina Becoming the Norm

Of the predictions as well, and this is something that again, we are born at a time and place where we never think twice about it. But our Prophet SAW predicted that, intercourse outside of marriage would become the normal. That Zina would become the norm.

Now, again we are born in a time and a place where it is the norm. So, we kind of think that this has been the case always. Now, even in Jahiliya, even in pre-Islam, families with dignity, and with respect, did not engage in premarital, much less extramarital.

And that is why, in the famous hadith of Sahih Bukhari, when the conquest of Makkah took place, and grudgingly Abu Sufiyan and his wife Hind accepted Islam. When Hind embraced Islam, she wasn't too happy. But she did it, then Allah SWT opened her heart for Islam.

So, she came to give the oath of allegiance to the Prophet SAW. It is a famous story, and many things happened there. Hind objected to every condition in the oath of allegiance. So, the conditions are going forth and Hind has something sarcastic to prod back.

One of the conditions was that, once you embrace Islam you will not do Zina outside of marriage. You will not have intercourse outside of marriage. Now, Hind was not sarcastic at this phrase. On the contrary, she was shocked. She said, "What type of condition is this? Does any free lady of dignity commit Zina? That you have to put this condition on us?"

In other words, even though she is not a Muslim at the time, and she's lived her life in pre-Islam, the concept of intercourse outside of marriage was unimaginable for her. That how is it even possible, that a dignified lady will do this? This was the perception they had pre-Islam.

And again, I'd like to remind us, in this land, you will be shocked to find out that, all of these trends go back one generation. Back in the 30s and 40s, and the people from that time that are still alive of this land, in their age, if somebody wanted to marry one another, then the man would have to ask permission from the father of the lady to go out on a date.

And the date would be chaperoned. And the goal would be not just floating around. No. This would be a marriageable age. The man has a job. They both are of right age. The goal is to see if they are compatible. This is back in the 40s and 50s. Norm of Zina was impossible to conceive in that era.

That's why, if a lady became pregnant outside of marriage one generation ago, it was a matter of shame for that family. This is literally one generation ago. Things have changed completely from the 60s and second wave feminism, and the radical sexual liberation movements.

All of this changed in the late 60s, early 70s. Before this point in time, even in this land, and all of the Western world, they had remnants of Haya. They had remnants of dignity and decency. Then everything has changed in one generation.

So much so, that these days if a young kid in high school is not dating, the council will have a conversation, "What's wrong with you? Is everything okay? Why aren't you doing this?" And statistics Wallaahi are depressing.

And we have to be blunt. We have to see these statistics. We need to understand that our children are living in this land, and they're facing these problems. If we don't solve them, where else do you expect them to be solved?

So, over 75% of teenagers, of both genders in this land are engaging in intercourse. Stop deluding yourself that your child is an angel. Your children are living in the same land. May Allah SWT protect all of us. We need to be aware of this.

There is a study done by a Canadian institute on the drug and sexual habits of Muslims on college campuses. It is the most thorough survey done of our Muslim community. And we have an endemic crisis. It is sufficing to say that it is terrifying. The survey says that college going Muslim boys and Muslim girls are involved in drug use, tobacco use, alcohol and Zina.

This is the world we live in. Now, this could never have been predicted even a hundred years ago. Even a hundred years ago, no one could have predicted this type of revolution. Because these families, the same people that were living amongst, they had Haya as well.

In this land, they had strict laws. Men and women aren't going to be together in public. They're not going to go out on a date, unless it is meant for marriage purposes. There was no such thing as casual dating. All of this has changed. And our Prophet SAW predicted that Zina would be everywhere.

Fahisha Becoming the Norm

The Prophet SAW also predicted that nudity would be everywhere. That Fahisha would be everywhere. That people would show their bodies in public. And again, these are things we don't understand. But in this country, in our own generation, the issues of pornography have changed radically.

Then there was an appeal in the Supreme Court, that overturned the ruling and in one generation from it being illegal to get a magazine, now pornography is ruining in every household in this land. And we still are reeling from the damages because of the internet.

Who could have predicted this? One generation ago, the government had a special body to monitor Hollywood. And any scene that was deemed to be immoral was cut off. That is why you will not find nudity in black and white movies. Because our own government had some Haya.

And Subhan Allah, in the 30s and 40s, if it showed drug use, or extramarital affairs, the movie would have to show that the people who did it, suffered. Because they wanted to teach morality. They wanted to demonstrate that drug users don't end up happy. They wanted to demonstrate that extramarital affairs have problems.

This is in this land. That's why if you look at the 40's, every day, all of these famous people, their movies overall had a positive image. Not that negative. Nowadays, even on Disney Channel, you have material that is not fit for children. When I grew up, Disney Channel was relatively innocent. We all grew up in a different era.

Now, on Disney Channel, every second joke is with a sexual innuendo. Every second thing is about boyfriend and girlfriend. Who could have predicted this that things will change in just one generation?

Our Nabi SAW predicted it. He predicted it in an era, a time and place, where no one could have imagined that nudity would be prevalent. The prophet SAW said that, "Fahisha is going to be the norm". The hadith is explicit and is authentic.

The Prophet SAW also said that, "A time will come when copulation will occur in public, like donkeys do in public". And the way things are, we are even less than one generation away from this as well. May Allah SWT protect us.

The Prophet SAW said that, "And there will be a man, who will see this happening, and he will say to them, 'Couldn't you get a room'; 'Couldn't you go behind the door or a wall'. And that man will be deemed by them, to be so righteous, the way you look at Abu Bakr Siddiq".

Now, if you look at where this society is heading, I swear it is terrifying. For teenagers and for youngsters, this seems to be the norm. Those who have grown up in the 70s and 80s, will tell you how quickly things have changed. In our own lifetimes, in one generation, it has begun to exponentially change. It's not changing steadily. No, it's exponentially changing.

Also, that explains the rise of weird manifestations of sexual habits which we're seeing as well. Because this is what happens when you open this door. Our Prophet SAW predicted this. He mentioned that, "Towards the end of times there will be a lot of women, who are clothed, and yet they are naked".

In other words, they're not dressed properly. And He said, "They will love to entice others. And others will love to be enticed by them". In other words, what this means is that, flirtation is open and sexuality was open. Our elders you don't know what tinder is.

This is exactly what tinder is. This is now open without even Haya. Haya itself is gone. This is explicitly predicted by the Prophet SAW that, "Of the last things to be gone from mankind will be Haya. When Haya is gone, wait for Judgment Day".

Proliferation of Intoxications and Music

Of the things predicted by the Prophet SAW is the proliferation of intoxications towards the end of times, and the proliferation of music as well.

Now music existed in the time of the Prophet SAW. But it wasn't common, it wasn't the norm. Intoxicants existed, of course. But again, it wasn't the norm.

Our Prophet SAW came and forbade intoxication and definitely discouraged the issue of musical instruments. And he predicted that a time will come when this will be the norm.

That it will be everywhere. And again, we see this now that the rise of marijuana and other things is now the norm.

It is something that unfortunately even our own youngsters, many of them don't think this to be big of a deal as well.

Empty Mosques

Of the trends that are predicted by our Prophet SAW is the building of Mosques, that will be empty. We seek Allah SWT's refuge from ever having Mosques that are empty. It is virtuous to have good Mosques. But we want them to be packed.

But he predicted that a time will come, when the Masjids will be magnificent and nobody will come to pray in them. We seek Allah SWT's refuge. But there are plenty of Masjids, that are empty at times. Especially in the oil-rich countries, you see in the middle of nowhere, just for the sake of showing, that a mosque is built.

And hundreds of millions are spent. But when comes to salah, it is empty; completely empty. That's not the goal of the sharia. Now again, you're coming to the Masjid, we would want the Masjid to be beautiful. Alhamdulillah.

The problem is not in beautifying the Masjid. The problem is in building the Masjid, for the sake of building it, and not for the sake of the people. When the Masjid is empty, that is a problem. And prophet SAW predicted that, "There will come a time, the Masjid will be beautiful, but the people will not be there to pray".

That is the exact opposite of the Masjid of the Prophet SAW. The message Nabawi was very, very simple when it was built. So much so, that there was no carpet. The Masjid had pebbles. That is why the Sahaba would not take their shoes off when they entered. They would pray with their shoes in that Masjid. Because they were praying on the sand, on the rubble, on the pebbles.

There was no roof on the Masjid. One time it rained and everybody became soaking wet. So, some leaves were put for a temporary period of time. In the whole lifetime of the Prophet SAW, there was not a solid roof on the Masjid Nabawi.

This happened in the reign of Umar Ibn Al-Khattab RA, that he decided to make some solid thatched roof. Otherwise, in the whole lifetime of the Prophet SAW there was no solid roof. Eventually they put an interlocking of leaves to protect them from the Sun. But not from the rain.

And that is why, even in one of the final Ramadan of our Prophet SAW it rained heavily, and the masjid became muddy. Anas Ibn Malik RA says, "Wallaahi, I swear, I saw the Prophet SAW lower his head into the mud in the 27th night of Ramadan. And he raised his head up and the mud was on his forehead".

In another narration it says 23rd Night of Ramadan. It was predicted to be Lailatul Qadr. The Prophet SAW was not embarrassed or shy to put his head down for the worship of Allah Subhana wa Ta'ala. No one is honored, more than the one who lowers his head to Allah Subhanahu wa'ta'ala.

The point being, the Prophet SAW predicted this issue of beautifying the Masjids, while neglecting the people in the Masjid. And Anas Ibn Malik RA commented on this hadith of the Masjids. And he said, "A time will come when people will boast about the Masjid, but they won't visit it. They will boast about how beautiful the Masjid is. But they will not be inside".

Let us be honest, there are Masjids around the globe, that people do boast about them. They boast about how big it is. How beautiful it is. But not the quality of the people in it.

Children Being Disrespectful to Parents

Of the generic trends that are mentioned, this is one of those trends that again are very cryptic. In the hadith of Jibreel AS, our Prophet SAW said that, "Of the signs of Judgment Day is that the slave girl shall give birth to her own master".

This is one of the most famous cryptic predictions of Judgment Day. What does it mean, that a slave girl will give birth to her own master? This is one of those things again that has a lot of different opinions about what this implies.

One opinion is that, Islam will spread so quickly that people will lose track of who is a slave and who belongs to whom. Such that the children will then assume that their own mother is their slave. Therefore, what is the prediction here? The prediction is the quick conquest of Islam. The prediction is how quickly Islam was spread. That is the interpretation.

Another interpretation, which is the one of Hafiz ibn Hajar RA, that children will become dominant over their parents. I'll let that sink in amongst the parents. Especially those parents who have teenagers. And take some consolation that this is predicted.

And Ibn Hajar RA has predicted that children will become bossy and domineering over the parents. And if you would go to some households, you don't quite know who is actually in charge of what is going on. And in fact, this was commented on by Ibn Hajar RA 800 years ago. That the meaning of this Hadith is that the children will dominate and give the orders and be disrespectful to their parents.

These are the two main interpretations of this Hadith. Number one, that Islam will spread very quickly so we won't know who is who. Number two, that children will dominate over their parents. Allah knows best. But it looks like, at least from our times, our perspective, that it is the second one.

Proliferation of Shopping Centers

Of the predictions that are the general trends, that are predicted of the Prophet SAW is the increase in the number of markets, bazaars, and the increase of shopping centers. Now, were there not shopping centers in classical times? Of course, there were.

But typically, every city had one area. Medina had one area. Makkah had one area. It was the bazaar. and it was very rare for a mid-sized City to have two bazaars. It didn't make sense. There's the place, you go, you shop and you come back. So, to have multiple shopping centers did not make any sense.

And shopping centers and bazaars and Suk, generally speaking, our Sharia has mentioned that they are not the most beloved of places. Number one, because of materialism and dunya. Number two, because of cheating and lying. Number three, because of interest. Number four, because robberies will take place over there.

Number five, from the beginning of times shopping malls have been associated with the riffraff and the thugs and the ruffians and the flirtations that happens over there. To this day this is the way it is, just as it was back then. It's not a place of piety and Taqwa. That's why our Prophet SAW said, "The most beloved of all places of any city are its Masjids, and the most despised of any city are its shopping places".

So, if you need to go buy something, you go and you get what you were looking for, and then you leave. But to make that your socialization, this leads to a hardening of the heart. This leads to the love of the dunya. It's not healthy.

What's the point of this? So, our Prophet SAW predicted that the shopping centers would proliferate and again we see this in our times as well.

Widespread Obesity

Of the most amazing things that the Prophet SAW predicted, and hadith is in Sahih Bukhari, that, "Of the signs of Judgment Day, is that obesity will spread amongst the people".

This is exactly from Sahih Bukhari that widespread obesity is one of the signs of Judgment Day. What an amazing prediction. Now, if we go back even 200 years, or a thousand years, or a thousand five hundred years; nobody was fat. Anybody who is obese, is the exception not the rule.

The Romans, the Persians, the Indians, the Chinese, the Arabs; everybody was busy walking and doing things. Obesity was never a problem of a land. It didn't happen. There was always the one who was very spoiled rich. But as a trend, it did not exist in any land. Think about that.

For our Prophet SAW to say that obesity will be a global trend, this is mind-boggling. No one could have imagined that there's going to be a World Health Council about the problem of obesity in the modern world. No one could imagine that the United Nations would have a department monitoring the obesity of countries.

No one could have imagined this even 50 years ago. Much less, a thousand five hundred years ago. But that is exactly what our Prophet SAW predicted that, "Obesity will be rampant in my Ummah and in all other Ummahs". And that is the reality.

Now, what does this mean? Is obesity Haram? Is it sinful to be overweight? Why is the Prophet SAW saying this? So, obesity is definitely not something that our Sharia encourages. We have to think that, is it something that Allah SWT and our Prophet SAW encourage?

Because what does obesity indicate? It indicates laziness, and gluttony. You're spoiled. You're giving up something else, which is your health. You're giving up being physically fit, being physically active. If you need to defend yourself, or your family, or your Deen, how should you be? Obese or fit?

A society that is obese, how can it defend itself when people are knocking doors down? So, being obese is not Haram. You're not going to go to Jahannam if you're overweight. Alhamdulillah, don't worry about that. But it's not something that Allah SWT and his Messenger SAW encourage.

That is why our Prophet Saw said that, "of the signs of Judgment Day is that obesity will be rampant". Everyone will be struggling with this. And out of the top ten countries, some are Muslim nations. We're all struggling with this. In some countries, Muslim lands, the majority of people and citizens are classified as obese.

And again, go back one generation. No one could have thought of this. One generation ago, the same oil-rich lands, they were struggling to get food. They were struggling for bread. Again, just because we're born in a time and place, we don't ever think back. That this same society, their fathers and grandfathers, were struggling for food.

Now, the tables have turned. Today, they have so much food that they're struggling, what to do with it. And this was predicted by our Prophet SAW.

Increase of Earthquakes

Of the predictions that our Prophet SAW made is that, there will be an increase in natural calamities and especially in earthquakes. That earthquakes would be on the rise.

There was a study that statistically compiled all the earthquakes of the last 500 years. This study was done by a non-muslim. They did mention that over the last hundred years, the frequency of earthquakes has actually increased.

So, this is now basically a fact, that between 11th century to the 18th century there were only about 64 earthquakes in the world. In the 19th century, there were about 47 earthquakes in the world. In the 20th century alone, there have been around 319 earthquakes.

And in a span of last 20 years, there have already been about 380 earthquakes. So, this is definitely one of the most remarkable signs that were predicted by our Prophet SAW about 1400 years ago. May Allah protect the Muslims and everybody in those reigns.

So, the frequency of earthquakes is definitely on the rise. And it is one of the signs of Judgment Day as well.

Ar-Rum as the dominant civilization

Of the signs of Judgment Day, is something that we are already seeing now. The hadith is a Sahih Muslim. The Prophet SAW mentioned that, "The day of judgment will only arise, when Ar-Rum are the dominant civilization of the world".

Who are the Ar-Rum? The word Ar-Rum literally means the Romans. And the Romans were a civilization, who by and large no longer exists as that race. But the western civilization, by and large, considers itself to definitely be the intellectual heirs of the Roman tradition. If not the biological heirs.

They pride themselves on ancient Roman and ancient Greece. And that is why, every one of us that has gone through their high schools and universities, when we start studying history, we start with their history. Not with human history. When we study the classics, who do we study? The Iliad and Odyssey by Homer, and we go back to Aristotle and Socrates and Plato. We start from there, then we work our way through the Renaissance, and then Newton, and then then we go through the Judeo-Christian side of things.

So essentially, this society is standing on two pillars. And those pillars are Judeo-Christian heritage, and Greco-

Roman Hellenistic heritage. The melding of those two is what has produced western civilization. And therefore, it is not at all a stretch to say that when the Prophet SAW said Ar-Rum, he was talking about the modern West.

This is a no-brainer. And he predicted that Ar-Rum will be the dominant civilization of the world. And once again when he said this, Europe was nothing. Europe was backward. They were called barbarians. The Arabs considered the Germans and others to be barbarians.

So, the Europeans of that time were not flourished. London, in the time of the Prophet SAW barely had 3,000 people. Europe was rising. And as for North America, there was nothing. So, what happened? Ar-Rum began to be more and more and more popular.

And with the collapse of the Byzantine Empire in 1453, this allowed the Latin Empire which is Ar-Rum to start coming on the rise. Because before 1453, Europe was always in the shadow of the actual Byzantine Empire, which was in Constantinople.

It was only after that, that they finally could claim to be the dominant civilization. Then of course, slowly Europe continued its ascent, until Ottoman lands and European lands were fighting one another on equals footing in 15th and 16th century.

Then in 17th century the decline begins and in early 1800s Ottoman lands become the sick man of Europe. Then the Muslims take a fall, technologically. But never theologically, and never morally. Never short sell yourselves, Muslims. We are the dominant when it comes to Akhlaq. We are the dominant when it comes to Akedah. We are the dominant when it comes to belief in Allah SWT and his Messenger SAW.

But technologically, Allah SWT tested us. Once upon a time, Muslims were dominant technologically. But things changed, particularly when the Ottomans began to go down, and Europe came on the rise. Now we see the tables have turned. And this is the first time that the global civilization is Western.

300 years ago, no one could have predicted which civilization would be the dominant. We were both on par with one another. But then that changed and one civilization rose and this leads us to the terrifying notion that this might be one of the precursors of Judgement Day.

Because for the first time since the original Roman Empire, the heirs of the Roman empires have now risen up from the ashes. And they are the dominant civilization of the world, as predicted by our Prophet SAW.

Prevalence of Kitabah

Of the predictions of the Prophet SAW as well, of the trends that are given; and again, this is very interesting. Because it's impossible that what we are reading would have been predicted by a false Prophet, Nauzubillah.

The very notions that are coming, indicate that the one who said this, Allah SWT is communicating with him. No one could have imagined what the Prophet SAW predicted is going to happen. And we are seeing it over here.

And of the things he predicted is that writing would become prevalent. Literacy rates would be high. Once again, who could have predicted it?

When the Quran was revealed in Makkah, the city of Makkah probably had around 2,000 people. Of those 2,000, probably less than a dozen could read and write. That's less 1%.

And our Prophet SAW predicted, "The signs of Judgment Day is Kitabah will be prevalent". Remember that most of the Sahaba could not read and write. Because that was the society. That's the way they were.

To predict that reading and writing will become the norm, not just in Muslim lands, but in the globe, is once again beyond even understanding. And this is exactly what he predicted.

Prevalence of Ignorance

Now another prediction seems to contradict this prediction of prevalence of Kitabah. The hadith of Kitabah is in Musnad Imam Ahmed. And the hadith for this prediction is in Sahih Bukhari.

The other prediction is that, one of the signs of the end of times is that ignorance will prevail. That Jahiliya will be everywhere. Now, how can ignorance prevail and at the same time the Prophet SAW was saying reading and writing will prevail. Is this a contradiction?

The response is that each hadith is valid. But it applies to different things. When the Prophet SAW is saying that ignorance will prevail, he's not talking about reading and writing. He's talking about knowledge of right and wrong. He's talking about common sense. And when he's talking about Kitabah, he's talking about literacy.

Before the rise of the internet, those of you who witnessed that era, in the 80's and 90's, mankind imprudently believed that if only we could give people access to education, they will all become intellectuals.

The internet came, and all of Encyclopedia, Britannica, Wikipedia became free of charge. Any database, any journal is there. But mankind instead of becoming more intelligent, it has taken a nosedive beyond that. This is what our Prophet SAAAW is saying.

That Kitabah will increase. Jahiliya will also increase. It's not a contradiction. Now, just because you're reading, therefore, it does not necessarily mean that your intelligence will increase. And we see how facts are treated as opinions and vice versa in today's time. This is what the Hadith means.

In last few years we have witnessed how the distinction between fact and fiction is blurred. And how ignorance is promoted against basic facts, and even scientific facts. All of this is a testament to what our Prophet SAW predicted. So, there is no contradiction in that.

The Mahdi

Now, we move on to the final of the minor signs that our Prophet SAW predicted, and that was the coming of one man and his name will be Mohammad Ibn Abdullah. And he will be called by the people the rightly guided, which is the Mahdi. And he predicted it in over 30 hadiths.

So, the Mahdi is not his name, it is his title. And it comes from the root word which means to guide. It's the opposite of delusion. The Mahdi means the one who is guided.

The Prophet SAW said, "If there were only one day left of this world before the Day of Judgment, Allah SWT would make that day long. He would stretch it out. Until Allah SWT sends a person from my progeny, from my Ahlal Bait. His name shall be my name. And his father's name, shall be my father's name." Therefore, the name of the Mahdi will be Muhammad ibn Abdullah.

So, the Prophet SAW continues, "He shall fill the earth with justice. As it was filled with Zulm and injustice". Ibn Al Qayyim RA, the famous student of Ibn Taymiyyah RA, said that, most of the traditions mentioned that, he shall be from the progeny of Hasan Ibn Ali RA, and not from Hussein RA. And that this has a very beautiful hikmah and wisdom.

He says that, "Because Hasan RA give up the khilafa for the sake of Allah SWT, Allah SWT will return the khilafa to his progeny". And Allah SWT knows best. So, he is saying that when Hasan RA gave up the khilafa, it is only befitting that as Prophet SAW said, "When you give up something for the sake of Allah, Allah will give you something better than that."

So, when Hassan RA gave up the khilafa of the Muslims, his progeny shall get something better than that, which is the khilafa of the entire world. The Mahdi shall rule the entire world. Unlike the Umayyad, and even if Hussein RA had been the Khalifa, he would have ruled a small portion of the earth. At that time, the Muslim Empire was only to Iraq, Syria, and Egypt.

Another aspect that the Prophet SAW told us, is that the Mahdi shall have a certain physical characteristic. The Prophet SAW said, the hadith is in the Mustadrak Al-Hakim and also the Sunnah of Abu Dawud, that, "The Mahdi shall have a large forehead, and he shall have an aquiline nose". Meaning a nose that is slightly pointed and long. In the Arabs, they consider it a sign of beauty and perfection.

So, these are the characteristics, that the Prophet SAW told us the Mahdi will look like, and this is not how the Prophet SAW looked. Just like Ali RA said, "The Mahdi shall resemble the Prophet SAW in manners and custom, but not in looks." So, the Mahdi shall not look like the Prophet SAW.

Regarding his spiritual characteristic, the Prophet SAW said, it is reported in the Sunnah of ibn Maajah, that, "The Mahdi shall be from the Ahlal Bait. Allah SWT will rectify him in one night, will make him good in one night".

This is an interesting hadith, because it tells us that the Mahdi in the younger portion of his life, will not be as practicing of a Muslim as he should be. He will not be to the level that he is worthy of being. Something will happen, we don't know what. And in one night he shall repent. And he shall become, basically the most pious person on earth.

We also know that in the times that he will come, the Prophet SAW clearly said, that the time shall be of the worst of time. That the entire earth shall be filled with evil and injustice. And that is something that very rarely happens. That you see fitna and fasad in the entire earth.

And the Prophet SAW said, "From the beginning of time until the Day of Judgment, there is no fitna that is more sever to mankind than the Dajjal". And when the Mahdi comes, in his life times, the Dajjal will come. So, we don't want to see that time. And we seek Allah's refuge from being alive at that time.

Now, we don't know when the Mahdi will come. But we do know where the Mahdi will come from. The location, the hadith mentioned in Ibn Maajah, and also, in the Mustadrak al-Hakim that the Prophet SAW said, and this is an authentic hadith that, "Three groups of people shall fight for your treasure. And each of these three leaders will be sons of a Khalifa".

So, three princes would be fighting, if you would like to use that word. The Prophet SAW didn't say princes, but sons of Khalifa will fight over your treasure. The scholars of hadith have said that the treasure being referred to here is the treasure that was buried underneath the Kaaba.

There is a major treasure buried underneath the Kaaba. We don't know exactly where it is buried to this day. It was buried by the tribe of Jurhum. It was buried in the ancient times before the coming of the Prophet SAW, by many, many, many, years. It was buried when the tribe was being attacked by neighboring tribe. So, they gathered all of their treasures, and they buried it in a location around the Kaaba. We don't know where.

So, three princes will fight over that treasure inside of the Haram. This will lead to a battle inside of the Haram. And the Prophet SAW said, "None of them shall win". They're not going to find this treasure, and none of them will win over the other two.

Then the Prophet SAW said, "There shall come black flags from the east. And then a war shall ensue between the Muslims, that the severity of the war, no ummah has ever under gone such a severe war".

So, he's saying black flags will come from the east, meaning the lands of Khorasan. Another narration, in Muslim and Imam Ahmad says, "When you see these black flags, realize that there will be the Mahdi."

So, the Prophet SAW didn't say that the Mahdi will be with them. He said, "There will be the Mahdi. So, when you see the black flags, give bay'ah to the Mahdi, even if you have to crawl on snow to get to him".

The Prophet SAW said, "When a Khalifa dies, sometime in the future, civil war will break out. And a person from my family, from the Ahlal Bait will leave Madinah."

So, the Prophet SAW mentioned that the Mahdi shall come from Madinah, running away from it, to Makkah. And he shall reach the Kaaba, and the people will force him out of his house, and give him the bay'ah between the Rukun and the Maqam.

The Rukun means the black stone. They shall give him the oath of allegiance between the black stone and the Maqam. The maqam is Maqam of Ibrahim. So, between the black stone and the Maqam there is the space of 7-8 feet.

The Prophet SAW said in this hadith, and this hadith is authentic and is in Abu Dawud; that, "A man shall come from Madinah, from my descendant, he shall flee, run away".

Which means the Mahdi will be scared, because he is being targeted, he's being hunted down. He shall run to Makkah, seeking protection in Makkah. He's in hiding, he doesn't want the people to know who he is.

And the people will take him out of his house, and give him the bay'ah between the Rukun and the Maqam. So, the Mahdi does not want to be the Khalifa. The people will force him into the Kaaba and give him the bay'ah.

Simultaneously when this occurs, the other hadith tell us that there's civil war taking place. Three sons of the Khalifa are fighting. So, in this civil war, the people turn to the Mahdi as the solution to the civil war. And when they give him the bay'ah, simultaneously a group of Muslims from Khurasan shall march towards the Kaaba. In order to help the Mahdi and become his army. And they shall have back flags as their banners.

Therefore, the Prophet SAW said, "When you see those black flags, that is the sign, this is the Mahdi". Scholars assumed and this is an opinion, that the Mahdi will be amongst the black flags. But this hadith tells us, the Mahdi shall be from Madinah.

So, correct opinion appears to be that, the Mahdi will come from Madinah to Makkah, during this time of civil war, and there will be many people claiming to be the Khalifa. The people will see the Mahdi and recognize him to be the Mahdi. And they will want him to be the Khalifa. So, they will force him to take the bay'ah.

And when this occurs, an army will march forth, and they will want to be the followers of the Mahdi. And when that army marches forth, that is the sign, the Prophet SAW says, "When you see that army, know that this is the Mahdi, give him the bay'ah, even if you have to crawl on snow to get there."

In this hadith from Bukhari and Muslim, the Prophet SAW said that, "I saw in a dream, something very strange. A group of people of my Ummah will intend to attack the Kaaba. Because a man from my descendant, from the Quraish has sought refuge in it. He has turned to the Kaaba, he has sought refuge in it, and he was running away from this army."

So, an army of Muslims will intend to attack the Kaaba, to attack the Mahdi, and as they are camped outside of Makkah, at a place called Al-Bayda. And to this day outside of Makkah, there is a suburb called Bayda. When they are camped at Bayda, Allah SWT will cause the earth to open up, and swallow the entire army.

This hadith is in Bukhari and in Muslim. And it does not mention the Mahdi by name. But it says, a man from the Quraish, a man from my progeny, meaning the Mahdi.

Aisha RA asked, "Ya Rasool Allah, there are people in the army who are not intending to attack." Meaning there are people who are just traveling along. The Prophet SAW said, "All of them shall be destroyed, and on the Day of Judgment, Allah SWT will see what their Niya was".

Beautiful hadith, because when this time happens, there will be many Muslims in the army who won't realize what is happening. They're sincere Muslims. All of this is in the will of Allah SWT, that Aisha RA asked this question, so that it be recorded for us as well.

There will be people who are forced to go. If they don't go, they're going to be killed or threatened. For Example, in some countries today, if a soldier doesn't do what he is told, he is court-martialed, and thrown to jail and is tortured in some cases. So, Aisha RA made an exception, for these people, that not all of them will be evil.

Another benefit that we have of the Mahdi, is that, he shall be the leader of the entire Muslim ummah. He is going to unite the ummah, after they were divided. And he shall enjoy the greatest khilafa ever known to the Muslims. Better that the Umayyad, better than the

Abbasid, better than the Ottoman, better than All of the other Khalifa that we've had.

The Prophet SAW said that there will come a time where the Mahdi will come, he shall give money to everybody and not fear poverty, and not even count it. And he said that food shall grow, and the crops shall produce, and everybody shall live in security and peace. This is after the Mahdi spreads justice after the injustice.

We also know that the Mahdi shall rule for seven years. The Prophet SAW said in the hadith in Abu Dawud that, "He shall rule for seven years". So, the time period of the Mahdi is not very long. There will be fitna and turmoil, the bay'ah will be given to him, and he will become the Khalifa. After he becomes the Khalifa, there will be seven years of perfect justice. It shall be the best seven years of the time the Muslims have ever enjoyed on earth. But then, Dajjal will come.

The Prophet SAW predicted, and our scholars mentioned, that the Mahdi is the final of the minor signs of Judgment Day. And the Mahdi will be a link, or a bridge, between the minor signs and the beginning of the major signs. The beginning of the major signs will be the coming of Dajjal. That is the first of the ten major signs.

The Mahdi will be alive when the Dajjal comes. So, the last of the minor signs, and the first of the major signs will coincide with one another. The Mahdi will see the coming of the Dajjal. The Mahdi will be in charge of the affair of the ummah, and he shall battle the forces of Dajjal. He shall be fighting the forces of Dajjal, fully knowing that he'll never defeat them. And that is very depressing. But he will have to do it.

He will fight the Dajjal. But he will not be successful. He knows he cannot kill the Dajjal. He knows it, because the Prophet SAW said, "Isa ibn Maryam is the one who will kill the Dajjal". But what else are you going to do? you have to defend yourselves.

So, the Prophet SAW said that, "The time will come when a leader amongst you, will be leading you in Damascus." Now, The Prophet SAW didn't say the word Mahdi. But in this case, it is the Mahdi. And he will be fighting basically the forces of Dajjal. And he will stand up to lead the Fajr prayer next to the white minaret.

The scholars say, this white minaret is of the Umawi Masjid, also known as the Umayyad Mosque. Which is one of the most ancient masjids, that is still a functioning masjid of the Muslim world. Built over 1,200 years ago, it has a huge white minaret.

So, he shall be leading the Muslims in Damascus for Fajr. And the Prophet SAW said that, when the iqama is given, before the Mahdi could say Allahu Akbar, the second of the major signs will come in front of them, and that is Isa Ibn Maryam AS.

As they're watching, they will see in the sky that, Isa ibn Maryam AS is coming down, and he shall be on the wings of two angels. The Mahdi will say to Isa As, "This is your prayer to lead, lead the prayer for us." So, the Mahdi will ask Isa ibn Maryam AS to lead the Fajr prayer.

The Prophet SAW said in Sahih Muslim, that, Isa ibn Maryam will say, "No. the iqama was given for you. So, you lead the prayer'". This hadith is a sign of respect to this ummah, that Isa ibn Maryam AS will pray behind one of the descendants of the Prophet SAW.

Then, the Mahdi will fight in the army of Isa AS. And then eventually Isa AS will be the one who kills the Dajjal. Then there is no mention of the Mahdi. Leading the prayer, is the last mention of the Mahdi.

We don't know anything more about him. What will happen to the Mahdi? Allahu a'lam. But, in some Zaeef hadiths it is implied that the Madi will pass away in the life of Isa AS, and that Isa AS will lead his Salat al-Janazah.

Analyzing Cryptic Hadiths

So, when we are teaching Islam these ambiguous hadith come up with cryptic predictions of Judgment Day. What is the best way to teach or approach these subjects? So, where the wording is cryptic, we should always narrate the wording and then say Allah knows best. That, this seems to be an interpretation.

We should never categorically say, this is what the Prophet SAW intended to mean. How do we know what he exactly meant? Let's take an example. One of the predictions of our Prophet SAW is that, "You will fight a group of people. Their eyes will be squinty and their faces will be flat like a shield".

Scholars have interpreted that to mean Genghis Khan. Maybe that is true. But I'll give you another example. The Quran mentions the coming of Ya'juj and Ma'juj. When Genghis Khan came, and he massacred everyone. There was blood everywhere, outside the city of Urgench.

He made a pyramid of a million Muslim skulls. He massacred the whole city and he made a pyramid of the heads of the women and children and men over there. The Muslims witnessing the conquest of Genghis Khan, they swore by Allah SWT that, 'This has to be Ya'juj and Ma'juj. Now we're just waiting for Isa AS to come, the

Dajjal to come, and Qiyamah to come. Because Genghis Khan is Ya'juj and Ma'juj".

So, all of the Hadiths about Ya'juj and Ma'juj, they applied it to Genghis Khan. And perhaps if we were alive back then, we too would have been certain that, we are seeing Ya'juj and Ma'juj. What else are you going to think? As it says in hadith that, "They are going to be coming from everywhere and you will not be able to overcome them".

The Mongols were exactly like that. But it turns out they weren't Ya'juj and Ma'juj. So, from this we learn, never ever take a cryptic hadith and then be certain that this is the correct explanation. So, as we mentioned that the Prophet SAW predicted, barefoot Shepherds competing with one another.

Now, in our times we see this happening. What if a generation later, an even more explicit example happens? Because right now the people competing, their fathers were barefoot shepherds. But how do we know? Maybe in next generation, literally something will happen and you will have barefoot shepherds doing this.

Then that generation will say that, this hadith is applicable in this situation. So, we can quote scholars, if the Ijtehad has been given. But always say Allah knows best, and leave cryptic hadith as they are.

Christian Interpretations of Second Coming of Jesus AS

The narrative of Christians, in their belief of Jesus AS' coming is one segment of Christians. Typically, Baptists and certain strands of evangelicals. These are the ones that are embracing the second coming of Jesus AS.

That is why you will find a group called Christian Zionists. These are Christians who are the most ardent supporters of Zionism. Because they believe that when the children of Israel are all gathered in the Holy Land, that is a necessary precursor for the coming of Jesus Christ.

That is why, some of the most ardent Zionist of this country are not Jewish people. They are people of a Christian background. Therefore, the Politicians, they flirt with Christian Zionists because they want their support.

So, their version of events is that, when Jesus will come, those who truly believed in him will magically disappear and be transported to heaven with him. And the wretched will be left on earth. And again, there are multiple interpretations of their version of events as well

So, they have this notion of Jesus AS coming back, gathering his followers and with his followers magically being transported to heaven. So, there's a very prominent series, one of the most popular readings amongst the Evangelic community, and it is a national bestseller, about those that are left behind, and those that didn't make it to be with Jesus AS. Because they weren't Christian enough.

So, the goal is you better be Christian enough, so that you're not left behind. And of course, they do believe in the Armageddon. They do believe in a massive war between good and evil. And that in the end Jesus AS is going to win.

Now, this leads me to an interesting point. A lot of times these people, they say that our hadiths mention war, bloodshed, Armageddon and violence. The response is very clear. We say to them this is going to be a war between Jesus AS and the Antichrist. If they want to choose to be on the side of the Antichrist, that's their business. But we're going to choose the side of Jesus AS.

We believe that Jesus AS will be our leader. When Isa AS comes back, he will be our leader and not theirs. That's why Allah Subhana WA Ta'ala says in the Quran, "Not a single person of Ahl Al-Kitab will be there, except that he shall believe in Jesus AS before Jesus dies".

Meaning, when Isa AS comes back, every Ahl Al-Kitab that had even an atom's weight of Iman, will become a Muslim at that time. And only those who had no Iman, will choose Dajjal over Isa AS.

Hadiths About Muslims Conquering India

Now, there are hadiths about Muslims conquering India. There are three traditions, to be precise, about the notion of Muslims conquering India. And those that conquer India will be of the greatest armies etc. However, all of them are slightly weak Hadiths.

So, Zaeef hadith can be used for encouraging, but they cannot be used for legal matters or theological matters. And belief in judgement day is theology. So, we cannot be certain. But I don't have any problem quoting them and simply pointing out that in some hadiths Conquest of Hind is predicted.

The Prophet SAW praised the army that will attack hind. But these hadiths have a slight weakness in them. So, we cannot be certain that the Prophet SAW said them. But we hope he said them. And especially for our Muslim brothers in India, they need some help. So, we hope that Inshallah those Hadiths are true.

Major Signs of Judgment Day

Now, we will cover the ten major signs of Judgment Day, one after the other. And we will begin with the one that we know is the first of the ten. And it is also the one that we have the most details about. And we'll discuss various opinions and issues and controversies surrounding this first sign.

Realize that not all of the ten signs the same amount if details available. For some we have a lot of details and in fact, for some of them, there are just a plain mention by name and no details what so ever are given. An example of this are the three earthquakes. That's all that we know about the three earthquakes. Not much is known about those signs, so we can just zoom in to them.

So, not all 10 signs have the same amount of details available for us. But the first of the 10 major signs, and no doubt the most interesting for most Muslims, also the most controversial, is the concept of Dajjal.

The Dajjal will be the first of the ten major signs of Judgement day. How do we know this? Because the Messiah, the coming of Jesus AS will be coinciding with the Mahdi. The Mahdi and Isa AS will be on earth at the same time.

Now as we said before that we don't have details on how and when the Mahdi will die. There are no narrations. We don't know, how will the Mahdi die. And what will his death be like. We do know that Isa AS will live for a few years. And there is no mention of the Mahdi. So, the assumption is that the Madi will pass away, and Isa AS will live.

And what will Isa AS do? Isa AS will fight and kill the Dajjal. Therefore Dajjal, the Mahdi, and Isa AS will at one point exist in the same timeframe. So, of the ten major signs, the first of them without a doubt will be that of Dajjal. This is how we know the first of the ten signs.

And what did our Prophet SAW say? He said, "When the first of them comes, the other will come one after the other". They will follow up like a domino. Once the first one comes, the other nine will zoom. So, we seek Allah SWT's refuge from even seeing the first one. And the first one is the most terrifying of them. And that is Al Maseeh Ad Dajjal.

Dajjal

To reiterate, the concept of the Dajjal has been narrated by over 45 companions. We have Hadiths about the Dajjal in every single book of Hadith without exception. The concept of Dajjal is something that the scholars call Mutawatir. Mutawatir is the highest level of Hadith narrations. It means that many people have narrated it.

So, in the case of Dajjal more than 45 Sahabah are narrating from the Prophet of Allah SAW. Now, we can't go over all 45 narrations by 45 companions about the Dajjal. It will take us a number of dissertations to go for all of them. In a nutshell, we will look at some of the characteristics of the Dajjal.

So, who is Al Maseeh Ad Dajjal? What do we know about Al Maseeh Ad Dajjal? First and foremost, what is Maseeh and what is Dajjal. The word, Maseeh is used for only two people in Islamic literature. Number one, the Maseeh is Isa ibn Maryam AS. And number two the Maseeh Ad Dajjal.

Now, in Abrahamic religions, folklore of the Judeo-Christian tradition, the both of them, they are called the promised Messiah, and the false messiah. So, in the Christian literature, you have the true Messiah and that's Isa ibn Maryam AS and you have the false messiah or the antichrist. So, they are called the Christ and the Antichrist.

The concept of there being two paired individuals, Jesus AS and anti-Jesus; Maseeh Ad-Dajjal and Maseeh Isa Ibn Maryam AS, this is found in Christian literature, and it is found in Islamic literature as well. So, both religious traditions agree on this.

As for the Jewish traditions, there is not that much about the Antichrist. There doesn't seem to be the figure of the Antichrist. There is only the figure of the Christ. Now, Maseeh means to anoint. What does it mean to anoint? In old days, when the King became the king, he would be anointed. They would put some holy oil or a special oil on his forehead.

When a Prophet became a Prophet, in the time of the Bani Israel, he would be taken to the River Jordan, one of their holy rivers, and he would be anointed with the water. The concept of baptism comes from this. That he's going to be anointed with the water. The anointment means to rub. And word for anointment in Arabic is Masaha, and the one who is anointed is called Maseeh. The Maseeh is the one who is rubbed.

So, Isa AS is called Maseeh, because John the Baptist AS, or Yahia AS was the person to give him this anointment. After Jesus AS, no one has been anointed by Allah SWT, by the command of Allah SWT, by the Baraka of Allah SWT.

So, Isa AS is the final one anointed, because there were previous Prophet AS that were anointed. But Isa was the special and the final, so he is called Al Maseeh Isa Ibn Maryam AS. As for the Dajjal, we do not know who will anoint him. Definitely not righteous people. But most likely, his followers will anoint him. And he will be the false anointed one.

Now, there is no explicit evidence about this, but It is said that perhaps the Yahood, who follow him will anoint him; thinking he is the real Maseeh. So, they will do the ritual to Dajjal, that was done to Jesus AS. The ritual will be given to the wrong one.

And the people will assume him to be Isa AS. But he is not Isa AS, he is Dajjal. So, he is going to be the false Maseeh, the Antichrist, Maseeh Ad-Dajjal. So, his title is Messiah. And his noun, not his name, his Laqab is Ad-Dajjal.

What does Dajjal mean? Dajjal comes from Da-Jal. And DaJala in Arabic means to mix up. It also means to deceive. But not a regular deceit. The worst type of deceit is called Da-Jal. There is no English translation for it. DaJala is to mix the worst evil, with the most righteous truth.

And the reason why he is called Dajjal is because, he shall mix the worst evil and he will put it in with the truth. He will say that he is Maseeh Isa Ibn Maryam AS. And this is a Da-Jal. Because Isa AS is a righteous man, and that Dajjal is an evil man. So, he will take an evil, which is that he is a liar, and he will say that he is the best of the best and that he is Isa Ibn Maryam AS.

Even worse than this, he will say that he is Allah SWT himself. And what greater Da-Jal, what greater deceit, what greater evil is there, than to say that he is Allah SWT? And he will claim that he is being inspired by Allah SWT. So, he will make all of these claims.

And by the way, the person from Qadian, in last century, he went through the same things. He first said he is Isa AS. Then he said he is inspired by Allah SWT. Although, he never claimed he is God. But this Dajjal will claim he is God himself. So, that is why he is called Dajjal. That he is deceiving the people. He is substituting the truth with falsehood. Because no one will mix truth with falsehood, in a more brazen manner, in a more blatant manner, than Al Maseeh Ad Dajjal.

And our Prophet SAW predicted that there will be many Dajjals. It is an authentic hadith reported in Musnad Imam Ahmed and other books, and there's a version of it in Sahih Muslim. Our Prophet SAW said, "There shall be after me, thirty Dajjals. Everyone will be claiming that he is a Nabi. And there is no Nabi after me".

So, we learn from this hadith that it's not just one Dajjal, but there are 30. There are 29 demi Dajjals, and there is one major Dajjal. Prophet SAW said that the sign of these false Dajjals is that everyone on them will claim to be a Nabi. But there is no Nabi coming after Prophet SAW.

From this we learn a principle, that anybody who claims he is a Nabi, is in fact a Dajjal. Anybody who claims to be a Nabi, you can call him **a** Dajjal. As for the last one, that will be the last of them, the 30th of them, that is **the** Dajjal. That is the worst of them.

There was one in America as well, named Elijah Muhammad, the founder of the Nation of Islam. He claimed that he is Nabi, and he claimed that Allah SWT inspires him. He openly claimed to be a prophet of god. He was born Elijah pool, then he changed his name to Elijah Muhammad.

He asked his people to recite the Kalema, "There is no God but Allah and that Muhammad is his Messenger". And by that he meant **he** is the messenger, as he called himself Muhammad. And then he said, that Whenever a Muslim says Muhammad, that is me.

Saf ibn Sayyad

Now, before we get to the Hadiths about Dajjal, there are two interesting aspects that are found in hadith literature, that confuse the average reader. In fact, they even confuse some of the Sahabah. So there still remains some element of confusion about the issue of Dajjal.

The first of them was that there was an individual who lived at the time of the Prophet SAW, whom even the Prophet SAW, for a period of time, didn't know if he is a minor Dajjal or is he that Dajjal.

This incident is mentioned inside Muslim and many other books of hadith. It as an authentic incident. Multiple narrations exist about a certain young man, who lived in Medina. He was from one of the Yahood tribes and he was a sorcerer, a magician. He had a connection with the Jinn. he would call the Jinn and he would pretend he knew the future. And he would foretell the future.

In our religion, anybody who pretends to know the future is a liar. And in our religion, anybody who invokes the Jinn, and calls out to the Jinn, this is a magician. He is a Kafir. We don't call up to the jinn. We don't do anything for the jinn. I have a book dedicated to this topic of Jinns and Black Magic, about this reality of how magician has a relationship with the jinn, which is a very scary, and interesting, and deep topic.

Realize, that it is possible for evil people to invoke the jinn. And when they do so, this is what we call magic. And that's why magic is haram. It is always haram to invoke the Jinn, because they want nothing but evil. Whoever does so, must sacrifice their Tauheed and get involved in Shirk.

Because the payments that evil Jinns accept, is your worship. That is the only thing the jinn wants. The Jinn doesn't care about your credit cards and your money. The Jinns want the same thing that Iblees wanted. Which is, as Iblees Said to Allah SWT in his arrogance that, "I am better than this creation. Let this creation bow down to me. Let this creation worship me". And if the Jinn gets this, in return the jinn will do some favors for you.

So, there was this magician at the time of the Prophet SAW by the name of Saf ibn Sayyad. Some say his name was Abdullah ibn Sa'id. Him and his Yahoodi tribes remained living in Medina for a number of years. Not all of the Jewish tribes were expelled. Some small families remain. And he was from of those tribes, that lived on the outskirts of Medina.

When our Prophet SAW migrated to Medina, Saf ibn Sayyad was a young child, and he was about to reach puberty. And that's when our Prophet SAW began interacting with him. And there are a number of interesting narrations about Saf ibn Sayyad.

Of them is this hadith from Sahih Muslim that, the Prophet SAW heard that there is this young child, who has these visions of the Jinn, and he predicts the future. So, Umar RA and the Prophet SAW they walked towards a group of children who are playing. And amongst them was Saf ibn Sayyad.

ibn Sayyad was not aware that the Prophet SAW was coming, until he was right behind him. And ibn Sayyad turned around, and the Prophet SAW was there. So, the Prophet SAW said to ibn Sayyad, "Do you testify that I am Rasool Allah?" So, ibn Sayyad said, "I testify that you are the Rasool of the unlettered people". He said it in a derogatory manner.

ibn Sayyad, who is 13 years old, then said to the Prophet SAW, "Do you testify that I am Rasool Allah?" What did we say, one of the signs of a Dajjal is what? That Dajjal claims to be a Rasool. And look at his arrogance. This also shows you that, this is what happens when you start getting involved in magic. You really become a very evil person.

And the Prophet SAW said, "I believe in Allah and his Messenger". That was his response. And the Prophet SAW said to Ibn Sayyad, "What do you see? What visions come to you?" Ibn Sayyad said, "I see two people come to me. One of them tells the truth. One of them tells lies".

The Prophet SAW said, "Rather the matter has been made confusing for you". Meaning both of them are telling lies. Then the Prophet SAW said, "I have a test for you. I have hidden something for you". And the prophet SAW was hiding a verse from the Quran. That the Prophet SAW had Just recited a verse of the Quran to the Sahabah before coming to Ibn Sayyad. And he's testing Ibn Sayyad.

Ibn Sayyad says, "I know Ilm Al Ghaib. I know everything". So, the Prophet SAW tested him if he could recite that verse that was recited to the Sahaba. And, parenthetically, any person who charges money to predict the future is betraying his own lies. If he knew the future, he would be investing in the stock market and what not, become multi-millionaire instantaneously.

So, this man he is claiming he knows everything. So, the Prophet SAW just recited a verse, 20 feet away from him. And asked Ibn Sayyad if he tell his followers, what was just recited. And this shows you that even though ibn Sayyad had contact with the jinn, the jinn are not all knowledgeable. Because, he could not recite the whole verse. All his Jinn heard was two words of the Ayah that were recited to the Sahaba.

So, the Prophet SAW told him, "Confine O enemy of Allah. You shall never go beyond your meagerness". And the Prophet SAW was never harsh to anyone, except to those who deserved it. Umar Ibn Al Khattab RA said, "Ya Rasool Allah, allow me to execute him. This is a Dajjal. He has communication with the Jinn. His penalty is execution".

And our Prophet SAW said, "If he is that Dajjal, you shall not be able to kill him. And if he is other than that Dajjal, you're killing won't benefit anyone". This hadith is in sahih Muslims. It is authentic. Now, Umar RA will not be able kill him if he is that Dajjal, because no one will be able to kill that Dajjal except Isa AS. And it is useless to kill a Dajjal.

Another hadith is that, once the Prophet SAW went to test Ibn Sayyad and he walked towards his house with some of the Sahaba, and he hid behind some date palms, trying to see Ibn Sayyad in a way that Ibn Sayyad would not see him. But Ibn Sayyad's mother saw the Prophet SAW in the distance.

So, she shouted out to Ibn Sayyad informing him of Prophet SAW'S position. Then there was some conversation, that did not result in anything fruitful. And that Ibn Sayyad continued to live in Medina, after the time of the Prophet SAW.

And a number of Sahaba swore by Allah SWT, that he is **the** Dajjal. And of them, was Umar Ibn Al Khattab RA and his son Abdullah Ibn Umar RA. Umar RA would make Halaf with Allah SWT that he is **the** Dajjal. Also, Jabir Ibn Abdullah RA, the famous Sahabi, he felt that Ibn Sayyad is the actual Dajjal. And a number of other famous Sahabah believed this as well.

Now, An-Nafi RA, who is the famous slave that was freed by ibn Umar RA, and he became a great scholar of hadith. When Ibn Umar RA died, An-Nafi RA became the Sheikh of Medina, and Malik Ibn Anas RA came to study with An-Nafi RA. And So, the golden chain of hadith that we should all know, Malik Ibn Anas RA from Nafi RA, from Ibn Umar RA came to be.

This is one of the most famous Isnads of Islamic history. And An-Nafi RA was a servant, a slave, whom Allah SWT honored with knowledge. This is what knowledge does. He was purchased as a young child, as a slave. But he was eager for Islam. He memorized the Quran. He memorized hadiths. And therefore, every book of hadith has him on the golden chain.

So Nafi RA said, "I heard from my master Ibn Umar RA. He said, 'Wallaahi, I have no doubt that Maseeh Ad Dajjal is ibn Sayyad'". And there's a famous narration as well, that is mentioned in Sahih Muslim. That once Ibn Umar RA met Ibn Sayyad in the streets of Medina, and he had a verbal fight with Ibn Sayyad. And he made Ibn

Sayyad very angry, and Ibn Sayyad walked away stomping.

So, Ibn Umar RA then visited the house of his sister, and our mother, Hafsa RA. And Hafsa RA had heard the news that Ibn Umar RA and Ibn Sayyad had a confrontation in the bazaar, in public sphere of Medina. This is after the death of the Prophet SAW.

Hafsa RA said to her brother that, "What is the matter with you? Why do you have to interfere with Ibn Sayyad? Why are you getting involved in this issue? Don't you know that the Prophet SAW said that, the Dajjal shall come and appear, after something has caused him to become angry".

Meaning, 'Why are you poking him and prodding him? Why are you getting him angry? What is your business with the man? Let him be. We don't want that Dajjal to come when he's alive". Which means even Hafsa RA might have been concerned that Ibn Sayyad was Ad-Dajjal.

Now, this this issue of Ibn Sayyad being that Dajjal was denied by other Sahabah. And the most famous narration we have in this regard, is in Sahih Muslim. Also, parenthetically, Imam Muslim, he made a section in his Sahih about the hadiths about Ibn Sayyad.

Now this Hadith is narrated by Abu Saeed Al Khudri RA. And he says that, "One time I was doing hajj with Ibn

Sayyad". And in another narration umrah. So, it appears at this point in time Ibn Sayyad has accepted Islam. The Hadith continues, "and the time came for the caravan to stop". So, the caravans go for 5-10 hours, then they stop for the night, and the next morning they'll go again.

So, the time came to stop. And when the caravans basically stopped, everybody ran away from Ibn Sayyad. And Al Khudri RA says, "I was the one left next to him". Nobody wanted to be put his tent next to the tent of Ibn Sayyad. And he says, "I became very terrified of him, because of the rumors going around about him". Again, this is after the death of the Prophet SAW.

Al Khudri RA wants nothing to do with him. And he continues, "And looking around, he saw I was the only person there. So, he brought his belongings and he sat down next to me. I said to him, 'It is so hot over here. maybe it's better for you, if you rest in that shade over there'".

So, Ibn Sayyad stood up and he went over there. "Then, eventually some meat came to me. So, Ibn Sayyad stood up to share with that meat". Generally speaking, when you're in one Caravan, you're all going to share the meal. And nobody wanted to deliver the meal to Ibn Sayyad. So, they delivered it to Al Khudri RA. And Ibn Sayyad now wants to share that meal.

Al Khudri RA says, "He came and he sat down with me. And he had a glass of milk with him. He gave me some milk and he said, 'Go ahead take some'. So, I said, 'this milk is warm, and I don't like warm milk'. And the only reason I didn't want to drink it was because I did not want to touch anything he touched".

So, Ibn Sayyad said, "Ya Abu Saeed, how I wish that I could take a rope and tie it on that tree and commit suicide, because of what the people say about me". In other words, he knows exactly why Al Khudri RA would not sit next to him, and was not sharing the milk with him. And it's hurting Ibn Sayyad.

Then Ibn Sayyad said, "Ya Abu Saeed, don't you know by being from the Ansar, what the Prophet SAW said? Ya Abu Saeed, aren't you one of the most knowledgeable people about the hadith of the Prophet SAW? Ya Abu Saeed, don't you know that that Dajjal is a kafir and I am a Muslim? Ya Abu Saeed, don't you know that the Dajjal shall have no children, and I have left my children in Medina?"

So, Ibn Sayyad is now quizzing Abu Saeed RA. And by the way, these are all Signs. The Dajjal is a kafir. The Dajjal shall have no children. But Ibn Sayyad has children. Ibn Sayyad continues, "Ya Abu Saeed, don't you know that the Dajjal shall not enter Makkah and Medina? And here I am having left Medina, on our way to Makkah?"

Now he's giving some solid points here. How are you going to refute this? Now, one of the signs of Dajjal is that he shall not enter Makkah or Medina. And Ibn Sayyad is living in Medina and he's on his way to Makkah.

And Abu Saeed RA said, "He continued making these arguments, until I was about to have a soft spot for him". Then what happened? Then Ibn Sayyad said, "Wallaahi, I know who the Dajjal is. And I know, where he shall be born. And I know who his parents are. And I know where he is now".

That throws a spanner in all of this. Because how does he know all of this? So, Abu Saeed RA after having his heart softened, and feeling guilty; now all of a sudden, the terror comes back to him. And Abu Saeed RA says, "May you be cursed Ya Ibn Sayyad for what you have done". And then Ibn Sayyad walks away.

So, the topic of Ibn Sayyad is serious. There was some mistiness about him, and about who he was. However, eventually Ibn Sayyad simply disappears. We don't know when he died. The hadith goes that on the day of Harra, he just disappeared.

But clearly, Ibn Sayyad was not that Dajjal. Because he himself gave all of these signs that Abu Saeed RA had to acknowledge. Whether he died a Muslim or not, is another issue. Because Ibn Sayyad is claiming to be a Muslim, and the Dajjal is a kafir. And Allah knows best.

And this has caused a huge debate amongst the scholars. And Imam Al-Dhahabi RA in his monumental encyclopedia of the Sahabah, mentions a very interesting point. He basically says that, "Ibn Sayyad cannot be a Sahabi because the description of a Sahabi is someone whom the Prophet SAW met with, while that person was a Muslim. If the interaction occurred and the person was not a Muslim, and later embraced Islam, that person does not become a Sahabi".

And the examples or the possible example of this is Ibn Sayyad. Ibn Sayyad did not accept Islam in the lifetime of the Prophet SAW. If he accepted Islam, and that is a big if, that we don't know the answer to. If he accepted Islam, after the death of the Prophet SAW this does not make him a Sahabi.

Another interesting detail is that, the son of Ibn Sayyad became a great scholar. And his name is Amara ibn Saf ibn Sayyad. And this same Amara, is one of the teachers of Imam Malik RA. And Amara's name is found as a narrator of hadith. He is a famous narrator of hadith. And it is said that Imam Malik RA respected Amara immensely, because of his knowledge of hadith.

So, in summary, in the lifetime of the Prophet SAW, there was a cryptic figure who was a minor Dajjal in that time frame. And because he was still a young child, the prophet SAW did not know if he is going to grow up to become that Dajjal or not. And when the Prophet SAW passed away, that confusion still lingered on in the Sahabah. Some of them still thought that, he is that Dajjal.

But we now know that he could not have been that Dajjal. Now did he embrace Islam or not, Allah knows best. But this last phrase that he said to Abu Saeed RA means, he still had contact with the world of the Jinn. And he still has some issues that are un-Islamic. So, he dies in cloudy circumstances. And we leave his affair to Allah SWT.

Hadith of Tamim Ad-Dari

Now, the next incident of Dajjal. This hadith is in Sahih Muslim. It is the famous narration, that might seem to indicate that **the** Dajjal is alive and healthy as we speak. And that he is chained up in some mysterious island. And Allah knows best. What is this hadith? And where do we get it from?

This hadith is the famous hadith of Fatima bint Qays RA. One of the famous Sahabiyat. She narrates that, "One day we were sitting in our house. When we heard the crier running through the city saying As-Salat ul Jamia". As-Salat ul Jamia is how the Prophet SAW would call the Sahaba to the Masjid when there was an issue other than the five Salawat.

The Adhan is not given in this case. Rather this method of announcement is used. So, Fatima RA says, "I rushed to the Masjid to see what was happening. And I prayed with the Prophet SAW. And I was in the first line of the women, right behind the men, in my eagerness to hear what the Prophet SAW would say".

The point she's trying to make is that she heard directly, everything that Prophet SAW said. And she says, "After we finished praying, the Prophet SAW went on the Minbar and sat down, and he said, 'let everybody remain where he is. Now, do you know why I called all of you?'"

They said, "Allah SWT and his Messenger SAW knows best". Prophet SAW said, "I did not call you today to give you an advice or a sermon, or to cause you to cry, or to fear Allah. That's not the reason. But rather what Tamim Ad-Dari came to inform me".

Tamim Ad-Dari was one of the few Sahabah, who was a Christian and then embraced Islam. The majority of Sahabah were pagans. Very few were Jewish or Christian, when they embraced Islam. And of them is Tamim Ad-Dari. So, he was one of those groups of Sahabah, who were Ahlal Kitab.

So, prophet SAW says, "Tamim Ad-Dari came to me, embracing Islam, and he told me a story that happened to him, many, many years ago". Now, Tamim Ad-Dari is from one of the tribes up north. And those tribes were seafaring tribes. They would ride the ocean.

The Quraysh were a non-seafaring tribe. The Quraysh despised the ocean. The Quraysh did not like riding on the ocean. That's why, the Quran is full of references that the Quraysh did not like the ocean. And few of the Quraysh rode on the ocean.

That's is why, when our Prophet SAW, saw a dream, where some of his own Sahabah were riding the oceans, conquering other lands; he laughed, and he said, "I saw my own Ummah shall be riding on the waves, like Kings riding horses and steeds galloping, and they shall be conquering oceans".

And Uma Milhan RA a Sahabiyat, who was with the Prophet SAW said, "Ya Rasool Allah SAW, please make due that I am amongst them". Ans the Prophet SAW said, "You are amongst them". That is why she died and is buried in Cyprus.

Unlike Quraysh, people of Tamim Ad-Dari, they were seafarers. They were people who were involved in naval expeditions. So, Tamim Ad-Dari, he came to embrace Islam. And he came in the 9th year of the Hijra. and he came with a delegation to embrace Islam. And when he came, he told the Prophet SAW about something that happened to him many, many, many, years ago; when he was a young Christian man.

So, when he told this story, the Prophet SAW then called the Sahabah, and said, "Here is Tamim Ad-Dari. Let me tell you, what he told me". Now, it's a very long hadith. and you will find it in Sahih Muslim. You've all heard of it.

And the story goes as follows, that Tamim Ad-Dari says that, when he was a younger man, he was in a ship of around 30 people, from the tribe of Jhuzam and Lukham. These are Christian Arab tribes up north, and he was from those tribes. And once a very severe storm came in the ocean, and for 30 days they were lost at sea. They had no clue where they were.

Until they came to a faraway ocean that they could not recognize. And they saw an island in the distance. So Tamim Ad-Dari and a few of them, took the smaller boat to go get some water and to go get some food. Every large boat has that small boat to go in. So, they took that smaller boat to go to that Island.

And when they landed on that island, they met a very terrifying animal. A beast that could speak to them. And this beast was unrecognizable. The Hadith did not describe it. It simply says a beast, that's very hairy and could speak. Tamim and his people saw this and they were terrified.

The beast said, "Come with me. I'm going to take you to my master". And they went in to this island and there they went in to this cave, where they saw a man larger than any man they have ever seen. And the man was tied up in a more severe manner that any man they had ever seen. And the man, then began to ask a number of questions.

And they were so terrified they just responded one after the other. Of the questions was, is the Sea of Tiberias still there? Is this well still giving water? Is this land still cultivated? And they answered yes to all. And the man kept on saying that, "A time will come when there shall be no water in that lake"; "A time will come when this well will be dry"; "A time will come when this land that you consider to be very beautiful and green, will be completely barren".

So, he's giving predictions of the future. Then he says that, "Has the Prophet been sent amongst Arabs?" And Although Tamim Ad-Dari at this time was a Christian, but he was an Arab. So, he knows the Prophet SAW has come. So, he says, "Yes, he has been sent. And he has come out from Makkah and he has settled in Yathrib.

He didn't call it Medina, because only Muslims called it Medina. For those 10 years, when Islam was spreading, Yathrib and Medina where the name of the same city. The Muslims called it Medina and the Munafiqun and the pagans called it the old name of Yathrib. That is why we are not allowed as Muslims, to call it Yathrib unless we describe that, this is the pre-Islamic name.

The Dajjal says, "Did the Arabs fight him?" They say, "Yes". So, he says, "Who won?" They say, "Sometimes he wins, and sometimes the Arabs win". He is talking about Uhud being a loss, even though Uhud was not a loss from our perspective. Uhud was a stalemate. It was not a loss. But the Quraish interpreted it as a loss.

Dajjal then said, "If there is good in the Arabs, they should follow him. And I will tell you about me. I am the Maseeh. And it is only a matter of time, before I am let loose. And when I am let loose, I shall visit every single city on earth in forty days. Except for Makkah and Madinah. For they are made Haram for me. Every time I come to them; the Angels will stop me".

Then, the Prophet SAW stopped his lecture. And he began poking on the Minbar, and he said, "Did I not tell you about the Dajjal?" And they said, "Yes you did". Now this hadith ends over here. This hadith is the famous hadith of Tamim Ad-Dari. Narrated by one Sahabiyat Fatima bint Qays. It is inside Sahih Muslim. And its chain appears to be authentic.

Now, this hadith has caused a lot of disagreement in the Ummah. Because it throws a spanner, in what we seem to know about the Dajjal. Other traditions mention that the Dajjal will come towards the end of times. They mentioned that he shall be born to parents, who were childless for many, many years. And they're making dua for a child. And they shall be given a child. And they will not recognize that it is the Dajjal.

The Hadith about Hafsa RA, that was mentioned before, says that the Dajjal will come out and appear, because of some anger issue. Something will happen that will make him angry and he will become Dajjal. Whereas, this hadith seems to throw all of that to the wind. That the Dajjal is alive and healthy. And he knows he's that Dajjal.

This leads us to a very deep issue, that is it allowed to problematize a hadith based upon the content and not based upon the chain? This question, should it be allowed for scholars to problematize a hadith? We are obviously not talking of an average person. But for the scholars who understand Islamic traditions; is it possible for the hadith scholars to problematize a hadith, because the content seems different?

And the vast majority of scholars said, "No". And for good reason. Because, if you open this door, then any one will come and raise questions on a hadith that they don't understand. And we have people like that in our times.

A very small handful of scholars said, "Yes. but with a lot of conditions". And one of those conditions is that the problematization should not come from your mind or logic or rationality. It should come because it seems to be clashing with other hadiths.

If the problem seems to come with a clash from within the tradition, that is different than when someone can't understand the meaning of a hadith. As Ali RA said that, "If the hadith and the Sharia were to be based on my Akal, the Massah over the socks, should be done on the bottom. But I saw with my eyes, the Prophet SAW do Massah on the top".

This a very beautiful tradition. If our religion were to be based on what I think, on my Akal, on my common sense, then when you do Massah during Wudu, we should do Massah on the bottom of the feet. That is the part that will be most dirty. But the Prophet SAW did Massah on the top. When it comes to the Deen, we follow Allah SWT and his Messenger SAW. Whether we understand it or not.

But, what if within the Deen itself, you have hadiths that seem to clash? In this case, it is not my mind. We have to now reconcile between this. So based on this issue, we have some great Ulema from the past and from the present. They did problematize this particular hadith. And of them, we have from the generation before us, the famous scholar from a hundred years ago. And that is Shaikh Rashid Rida.

Many of us are influenced by him and we don't even know it. His influence was so profound that he had an impact on a global understanding of Islam. He was without a doubt the most famous Alim of a hundred years ago. He died in 1935. In 1919, every intellectual in the Ummah knew him. And he influenced people as diverse as Hassan Al-Banna and Muhammad Nasiruddin al-Albani.

Rashid Rida was one of those who said that, this hadith doesn't make sense, in light of all of the other hadiths. Another great Sheikh Muhammad ibn Saalih al-

Uthaymeen, who was a very traditional scholar of hadith, he also said that, "I don't consider this Hadith to be authentic, even if it is in Sahih Muslim. Because it seems to conflict with other hadiths".

Now, it doesn't make sense that Dajjal is alive and healthy. It also doesn't make sense that if this incident occurred, and the Prophet SAW has called the entire city, still only Fatima bint Qays narrates it. And Allah SWT knows best. Ibn Taymiyyah RA, in such situation would say, "My heart is at unease with the authenticity of this Hadith. My heart is not comfortable. Because the content is not adding up".

And Ibn Taymiyyah RA was a very humble man, he would say, "But if the Prophet SAW said it, then I believe in it". And this exactly should be our approach as well. The hadith doesn't seem to make sense. But if the Prophet SAW said it, we believe it. So, we put this hadith of Tamim Ad-Dari in a footnote, and we will leave it at that. And Allah knows best.

But conventional interpretation by conventional Scholars like Ibn Kathir RA, and Imam An-Nawawi RA, they considered this to be authentic, because this is in Sahih Muslim. Then the issue comes, how do you reconcile this with the other hadiths about the coming of the Dajjal. That Dajjal shall be born at a later time; his parents shall be childless etc.

Then, you have two opinions. The first of them is that, time and space mean nothing to Allah SWT. He is beyond that. So, by miracle and will of Allah SWT, Tamim Ad-Dari got lost in a different time warp, and they traveled to a different time and place; and Allah SWT is capable of all things. So, they saw an image of the Dajjal projected from the future back to their time frame.

The other interpretation is that, Dajjal is in fact alive and healthy; and that he was born; and all of this happened in the past. And then he is being chained and kept as the hadith of Tamim says. And he shall be released in the future.

Now the issue comes that only hadith that mentions Dajjal, alive and healthy and in chains, is this one hadith of Tamim Ad-Dari in Medina. Every other hadith gives a different narrative. So, you have two different narratives. Can we reconcile the two? Most scholars try to do that. But it's a very difficult fit.

So, these are two important standard controversies that every advance student of knowledge is aware of. That is the issue of Ibn Sayyad and the issue of Tamim Ad-Dari.

All Prophets AS Warned About Dajjal

Now, with these controversies covered, what do the rest of the hadith mention about the Dajjal? Of the things that are mentioned in authentic hadiths, the Prophet SAW said, "Every single Rasool has warned his Ummah about the Dajjal from the time of Nuh AS. And I too shall warn you about the Dajjal".

Now, this is actually very interesting for us as Muslims. Because the Prophet SAW is saying that the concept of Dajjal is found in all previous traditions. And we find it very clearly in the Christian tradition. As for the Jewish tradition, it appears that they don't really have this concept of the false Jesus.

But some sects of the Jews have the concept of the false David. And Allah SWT knows best. But it appears to be that, because they took David AS or Dawood AS, as their main figure, the folklore remains about the false David coming. So, they took their main figure David AS, and they made a contrary figure of him.

That there shall be a false King David and Allah knows best. And this is a small segment of the Yahood. And the vast majority of modern Jews they have abandoned these types of narratives. The vast majority of them take these as folkloric traditions. In fact, many of them don't even consider their religious laws as binding anymore.

They are what they call modern or reformed Jews. And that's the majority of American Jews. There are three main Firqas of Jews in America. Number one, is Orthodox Jews. This is the smallest population. Around 10 to 15%. They are also the strictest and the literalists.

Number two, is conservative Jews. Maybe around 20 to 25 percent. But the majority are number three, reformed Jews. For reformed Jews, essentially there is no Aqidah that that they have to believe in at all. And there is no Shariah that they have to follow. They are more of a civilization.

So, one group of the Orthodox, that is very small in percentage has concept of the false King David. The group with majority believes these to be folklore. But the concept of the false messiah or the false David is there amongst one group. Now, where did it come from? The Prophet SAW said, "Every Prophet warned his Ummah".

So, the Prophet SAW believed that the Prophet Musa AS would have warned the Jews about Dajjal. And we believe this as Muslims as well. As for mainstream Christians, Baptist Christians, evangelical Christians, Protestant Christians, they firmly believe in the figure of the Antichrist.

Now, you have two ways of looking at it. Now, the very fact that two different civilizations and two different faith traditions, that have no causal relationship with one another, are saying the exact same thing means there must be a common origin. And that is Allah SWT.

Same thing goes for the great flood. That every single civilization in the world has the myth of a great flood. The Native Indians in this land they have a myth of a great flood that took place once upon a time. The Aborigines in Australia believe it, and they are the most disconnected of humanity. For 20,000 years they were disconnected from rest of the world.

They lived separately from the rest of humanity and they have the myth of a great flood. The Bible has the great flood. The Quran has the flood. The origin stories of ancient Babylon have the concept of great flood. Why do all of these civilizations have a great flood myth?

Because there was a great flood. Now, it is true the details are very different. But that's because when you pass a fact from one person to the other person, ten to the other person, details become distorted.

So, the fact that every single civilization, Judaism Christianity, and Islam, it has some notion of an evil entity that shall deceive mankind towards the end of times is that the hadith of our Prophet SAW is correct.

Dajjal Will Be One Eyed

In another hadith about Dajjal, the Prophet SAW says that, "I am going to tell you something about Dajjal, that no Prophet before has mentioned to his people; that the Dajjal will be deformed".

Our Prophet SAW mentioned that Dajjal shall be physically deformed. Multiple Hadiths say about him not being even up to the standards of a regular, normal human beings. And a number of things are mentioned about him.

Now, we have established that dajjal is mentioned in scripts of the non-Muslims, the Christians, and the Jews. That the Dajjal shall be born to a family that is righteous overall, and is praying for a child for a long time, and that the child will later turn on the parents.

This is something that is in their folklore. And we find it in our traditions as well. One thing we do not find in Christian folklore and Jewish folklore is that the Dajjal will be deformed. Subhan Allah. This is one thing that the Prophet SAW told us, that no other Prophet before told his people.

The prophet SAW said that, "Dajjal Shall be born, and one of his eyes will be deformed". That is not found in any of the Judeo-Christian tradition. This is a sign of Iman for us. Now is it the right eye or the left eye?

There is a difference of open ion amongst the Scholars. Because once again, an authentic hadith seems to potentially contradict another hadith. One hadith mentions his right eye will be like a grape and another hadith mentions the left eye will be like a festered putrid. Some Ulema say, that both of his eyes are going to be deformed. Although, it is commonly said that his left eye will be deformed. And Allah knows best.

So, the prophet SAW mentioned that one of the eyes will appear like a rotten grape. A grape that is left outside for a while, and it pops open, and there's a brownish area. It is disgusting to look at. That will be the eye of the Dajjal.

The Prophet SAW is saying, recognize that man when you see him. There will be one eye that will be open and evil and putrid and festered and disgusting. That is one of the signs of Dajjal.

To summarize, one or both of his eyes will be deformed. Scholars have difference of opinions whether it is right or left. But in all likelihood is it really just one eye. So, one eye will be festered and will be basically like a floating grape, as our Prophet SAW said.

Kaffir on Dajjal's Forehead

Of the Hadiths about the descriptions of the dajjal is that, Prophet SAW said, "Every Muslim with an ounce of Iman shall recognize the words kaffir written on the forehead of Dajjal".

Meaning, anybody who has an ounce of Iman will recognize the Dajjal. And they shall see the word Kafir written on his forehead. Just like you can judge a person by looking at their face, actions and body language, we can understand what kind of person that is.

For example, you look at someone and you think, "I don't trust that person to be honest"; "he didn't seem like a truthful person". That gut feeling or intuition you have, is what is being said in the hadith.

And our Prophet SAW said, "The illiterate person will read it just as well as the literate person". You don't need to be a literate person to even recognize the concept of the Dajjal.

Now this sign is a sign of Iman. It is not a physical or literal sign. Because the kaffir will see Dajjal and not see anything literally or physically written on his face.

It is something that Allah SWT will give to the believer. This hadith is talking about the eyes of the Kalb, the eyes of the heart and not the physical eyes. So, the Momin will see the Dajjal and will see written on his forehead kaffir. So, this is something is also authentically mentioned.

Now, the Prophet SAW did not see Kafir written on Ibn Sayyad. So, the minor Dajjals will not have Kafir written on them. Ibn Sayyad was a child at the time, and the Prophet SAW was testing if he is going to grow up and become that Dajjal. Because from the traditions we learn that the Dajjal will grow up in a regular household, and he will become the Dajjal in a day.

As Hafsa RA pointed out that something will happen to make that Dajjal angry, and then his dajjal will appear. Before that, he's just an evil person. And when that person's Dajjal comes out, that is when he will get all his powers. Now, if Ibn Sayyad had become the Dajjal, then Kafir might have appeared on his forehead. And Allah knows best.

Dajjal shall travel the whole world

Our Prophet SAW also mentioned that, "The Dajjal shall travel the whole world and will visit every city". Now, when the word Kul-Lu is mentioned in the Quran, it means everything or every city, or every issue. Some people interpret this literally, that every single small village shall be visited by the Dajjal.

we need to understand that the word Kul-Lu in Arabic does not necessarily mean everything. It can mean a lot of. It depends on the wording and context. We know this from the Quran and Sunnah. Allah SWT says in the Quran "The wind of the Thamud destroyed everything". But the wind did not destroy everything. The wind did not destroy the rest of the world, but only Thamud.

So, Dajjal will not visit every city, but most of the cities. And as we mentioned before, that the Prophet SAW said that, "The Dajjal shall not be able to enter Makkah and Medina. Angels will surround the Makkah and Medina as protectors". This hadith also proves this point.

Claim of Being God

Of the characteristics of Dajjal is that he shall claim to be the Messiah and then he shall claim to be the God himself. And our Prophet SAW explicitly said that, "the Dajjal shall claim to be the Rab, and know that you shall not see your Rab in this world".

So, the concept of seeing Allah SWT is valid. But not in this Dunya. So, the Prophet SAW linked the concept of seeing Allah SWT with Ad Dajjal. That you shall not see your Lord in this world, because you will see him on Judgment Day and in Jannah and in the Akhira, Inshallah.

Now when he said, "You will not see your Lord in this world", also means that anybody who claims to be God is lying. Nobody, that you will see, will be God in this world. And he also mentioned that, "I will tell you that Dajjal is one-eyed and your Lord is not one eyed".

It means that Dajjal will not even be a perfect human being. How can he be God? Even his imperfection is obvious. He doesn't even have two eyes. Prophet SAW said, "Your Lord is not imperfect. Your Lord Allah SWT is Jalla Jalaluhu". Meaning Allah SWT is perfect.

You will see the Dajjal and you will recognize him. He does not even have the regular capabilities of a human. Then how can he be god?

First Appearance of Dajjal

Our prophet SAW also said, and the Hadith is in Musnad Imam Ahmed and it is a Hasan hadith, that, "Dajjal will come from a city called Isfahan".

So, it is mentioned by name. And the Prophet SAW said, "Dajjal will come from the Yahood of the city of Isfahan, and many of his followers will be from that City. 70,000 of the Yahood of Isfahan will be his followers".

Therefore, we see from this that the dajjal, his background will be from the Bani Israel. And many of his followers will be from the Bani Israel. And in another Hadith, the Prophet SAW mentioned that, "Dajjal shall come between the lands of Iraq and As-Sham".

So, how do you reconcile this? Our Scholars have said that, he will first appear in Isfahan and he will make his first claim of being Maseeh in Isfahan. But he will get global attention, when he appears between Iraq and As-Sham.

So, there are going to be levels of his appearing outwards. There are going to be levels of claiming. His first claim will be in Isfahan, in the land of Iran.

Of course, there is an interesting footnote that, from the destruction of the first temple of Babylon, the first batch of the diaspora of the Bani Israel, they migrated to Isfahan; and to this day, there is a group from that religion, in the population of Isfahan.

To this day, from the first destruction of the temple from the days of Nebuchadnezzar. These are the Yahood of the diaspora. They are still a small group, that used to be much more in number before 1947. But of course, because of the creation of the country, many of them have migrated to that land.

So, in all Arab and Muslim lands, they become very small. But there is still a synagogue in the city, and there are still people of that Faith and tradition in that City. And our Prophet SAW said that, Dajjal will come from that particular land and that particular City and that particular race and religion. He will be from that people.

Reason People Will Follow Dajjal

Also, we learn in the authentic Hadith that, the Dajjal will come at a time of great chaos, bloodshed, hunger and starvation. Then, he will provide his followers safety and security. This explains why, so many people will follow the Dajjal.

If you think about it, Alhamdulillah, most of us have never been hungry to the point of us going almost mad. We don't understand that when you are hungry, you lose rational. When you cannot feed yourself, or your children, you will do desperate things. May Allah SWT protect us from ever seeing that day.

But the people of that time frame will be tested by trials of war, bloodshed, hunger and starvation. Then, there comes a man who appears to be powerful. He has an army. He will grant you safety and security, if you are on his side.

Our Prophet SAW said, that, "Dajjal will command the skies to rain, and they will rain". Our Prophet SAW said, "He will distribute bread and food". One of his signs is that, he will be giving food left right and center, at a time of starvation.

When people are starving, they are willing to do many things. He will demand his followers to believe in him, first as the Messiah, and many of them will believe in him. When they believe in him as the Messiah, he will then raise the bar, and he will say, "I am your God. I provide your food for you. I provide your drink for you. I give you safety and security".

So, his followers will then take him as a god; and he will, at that time frame give his followers food and drink. Many other people will not have the food and drink. So, people will begin to follow him in mass. And this is the Fitna of the issue of the Dajjal.

Control of Shayateen

Our Prophet SAW also said that, the Dajjal will have the Shayateen at his disposal. So, the Shayateen will do things at his command. And the Shayateen are able to do which we are not able to do.

Now, the Shayateen do not have supernatural powers. But they have superhuman powers. The two are different. Supernatural is not the same as superhuman. A horse has superhuman powers, in that it is faster than us. But it doesn't make it supernatural. An elephant has superhuman strength over us, but that is not supernatural power.

Jinns have powers that Allah SWT has given them. Once we understand their powers, there's nothing strange about them. The only thing that we should understand is that, they're in a world that we cannot see. Allah SWT says in the Quran that, "Shaitaan sees you from a dimension, you cannot see him".

So, the Jinn are faster than us, stronger than us and they're invisible. That's it. Many creatures are faster and stronger than us. We're not supernaturally scared of lions. We might have a natural fear of them. But we're not terrified of them, in the sense of a supernatural way.

Only difference between the lion and the Jinn is that, the Jinns are Invisible. That the Jinns are in the world of the Unseen. Otherwise, if we understand that the Jinn are faster and stronger. What they can do is they can lift more than a human can lift.

But even their strength is not supernatural, it is super human. They can lift may be worth 50 people can lift up. They cannot lift the whole world. They are faster than us. They can move at the speed of light. Other than that, there are a natural creation of Allah SWT.

So, these entities will declare their loyalty to the Dajjal. Once, they declare their loyalty to the Dajjal, they will willingly cooperate with the Dajjal. And the Dajjal will appear to be a very powerful, supernatural person. But in reality, he simply has some of the tricks and trades of the Jinn.

The Jinn will make allusions. The Jinn will lift things up. And the people will not see the Jinn. The Dajjal will say, 'Do this', and something will happen; and the people will assume that it is the power of the Dajjal.

Dajjal Will cause the Sky to Rain

So, it is also possible, that Allah SWT will test the People, by giving the Dajjal one or two characteristics, that others do not have. Just like Allah SWT has given Iblees himself a long lifespan.

Didn't Allah SWT give Shaitaan something that we do not have? That is life until Judgement Day. No other person has that. No other person, no human being has that. And Allah SWT gave it to Shaitaan, as a test for Shaitaan, and as a test for us as well.

So, it is possible that Allah SWT will give the Dajjal certain privileges and powers, that are a test to him and are a test to those who follow him and will be a sign of Iman for those who reject him.

Of them, is the power of the capability to cause the sky to rain. Because the Jinns don't have that power. Jinns cannot cause the sky to rain. Only Allah SWT can do that.

As Allah SWT says in the Quran, "Who is the one who sends the rain from the heavens? Only Allah SWT". But Allah SWT can give that power to Dajjal.

Power to Resurrect the Dead

Also, the Dajjal will have the power to resurrect the dead. He will be able to do that at least once. Maybe more than once, but the minimum is once. And that is another thing that he resembles with the true Messiah and that is Isa ibn Maryam AS.

That's why he is the false Messiah. There are certain things in common. But Isa Ibn Maryam AS said, worship Allah; and the Dajjal says, worship me. That's why, he is the Dajjal. So, for sure he will resurrect one person at least, from the dead.

But in all likelihood, he will pretend to resurrect other people from the dead. This is explicit. It is mentioned in Sahih Muslim, that a person will come to Dajjal and will not believe in the Dajjal. And he will be a person, who doesn't know about Quran or Sunnah.

Dajjal will say, "What if I resurrect your parents in front of your eyes? And what if, your parents tell you to believe in me? Will you believe in me then?" So, he says, 'Of course, if my parents come and say it, I'll believe".

Then, Dajjal will command the Shayateen to take on the forms of the parents of this person. Shayateen can come in other forms. So, there's no such thing as ghosts wandering this world. The Ruh does not remain in this world. The Ruh moves on to the other world.

But what can happen is that, the Jinn can take on the form of a person. So that, when you see that entity, you think it is that person who has died. But it is not that person who has died. The person who has died is gone. That's it. They're not going to come back. But the Jinn can take on the shape from that person.

So, the Dajjal will tell the Jinns to come in the form of the parents of that person, and the person will then see his own mother and father. He will think that they're in the flesh. But they are not in the flesh. They are Jinns.

And his mother and father will say, "Oh my son, this is your Lord. Worship him". So, the naïve, innocent man will think that, his mother and father have spoken. That Dajjal is god himself and can resurrect the dead. Then he will believe in him.

Jannah and Jahannam of Dajjal

The Prophet SAW has warned us, that Dajjal will have tricks and trades. The Prophet SAW also said that, Dajjal will have with him, Jannah and Nar. Some scholars have said, it literally means a fire and a garden. Some scholars have said, it means that he will come with things that appear to be blessings, and lots of punishment.

Both are allowed here. Because Jannah represents money and fruits and sustenance. And Nar represent punishments and torcher. So, it could be that, he actually has a physical Jannah and Nar. And it could be that, what the Prophet SAW is saying, because the Arabic allows this, that it might be metaphorical and not literal.

Jannah indicate luscious gardens. It can indicate lots of fruits and pleasures. So Dajjal will have with him pleasures, and he will have with him punishments and tortures. So, our Prophet SAW said that, "Realize his pleasures are actually his torture; and what you think is his tortures, is actually Jannah".

And the Prophet SAW said that, "If one of you sees him, and cannot escape; then he should jump into the punishments and that will save him". So, if you have real Iman in Allah SWT, when you see Dajjal and he has his torture mechanism, he has entities that you think will harm you, will kill you; The Prophet SAW said, "Jump into what you think is harmful and you will be safe".

Now, it is possible, and Allah SWT knows best; that this Nar that you see are Shayateen, and when you jump into them, you are demonstrating Iman in Allah SWT. And the only way to fight the Shayateen is through Iman.

You cannot fight them with your fists. They are stronger than you. You cannot take them down with your physical strength. The one thing that you have, that will diminish the Shayateen is your Iman in Allah SWT.

Our Prophet SAW was on an expedition. The Hadith is in Abu Dawood. Where a certain person's camel went upward and almost threw the person off for no reason, in the middle of the desert. So, the Person said, "May Allah SWT curse Shaitaan. Shaitaan caused my camel to do this".

The Prophet SAW said, "Do not mention Shaitaan like that, because if you do this his ego will become so big, he will become bigger than a house. Because you ascribed this to Shaitaan. Rather say Bismillah, and when you do so Shaitaan will become smaller than an ant".

What was the power that was used? The name of Allah SWT. So, Iman caused the Shaitaan to become insignificant. It is possible, it's not too much of a stretch, to say that, Dajjal will have instruments of protection. Or what looks like protection. Like food and drinks. And he will have instruments of torture and evil.

When the people see, they will be terrified and they will rush to the gardens. Thinking that, that's going to save them. But that's going to destroy them in the Akhira. Our Prophet SAW said, "If you have no choice, you have between the garden and the fire; then jump into the fire of the Dajjal".

It is very possible. It's not a stretch. This torcher of the Dajjal might actually be physical. Could be armies of evil people, Jinns and Shayateen. And if you jump into it, putting your trust in Allah SWT, you will go unharmed. That everybody will run away and you will be safe. Because your Iman in Allah SWT will save you. So, this is the test of Iman, when you see the actual Dajjal.

Other Hadiths About Dajjal

Young Man

So, Dajjal shall be from the children of Adam AS. This is also clear from Hadiths. Another sign is that, the Dajjal will appear like a young man. He's not going to be an old person. He will appear like a young man between twenty to thirty years old. He's not going to be fifty or sixty or seventy years. His facial features will be that of a young man.

Curley Hair

Another sign that the prophet SAW mentioned was that, "The Dajjal will have curly hairs". So, he's not going to have straight hairs.

No Children

Of, the things mentioned about Dajjal is that our Prophet SAW said that, "Dajjal shall have no children".

Crooked Legs

Of the things that are mentioned as well about Dajjal is that, "He shall walk with crooked legs". His legs will be basically not be straight legs. So, this is another deformity. That he will not be walking normally. All of these are meant to emphasize that the Dajjal is a person who has physical imperfections. And yet in his arrogance, he is claiming to be God himself.

Eastern land

In one Hadith in Tirmidhi, our Prophet SAW said that, "The Dajjal will come from an Eastern land that is called Khurasan, and groups of people will follow him. They will be as if their faces are hammered out shields".

By a shield that has been hammered out, it means their faces will be flat. Now some have said that these are the description of the Eastern folks. And Allah knows best.

But the point is, there facial features will be something that is atypical for the Arab race. The Arabs will not find them to be of their race. The majority of people that will follow him will be from that other race.

Dajjal Will be Ahmar

Also, our Prophet SAW describe the Dajjal as being Ahmar. What does Ahmar mean? The Arabs of old, they would call Ahmar, which we call in modern vernacular Caucasian. They would call them reddish or yellowish. Ahmar or Azfar was the term the Arabs used to describe the Caucasian types of people.

So. when the Hadiths mentions any Nation or race as being yellow or red, this is our equivalent of that complexion. Now, the Prophet SAW described him as Ahmar. And again, it fits into the description of the ethnicity of the Dajjal.

Description of Dajjal

The Prophet SAW said that his hair will be curly. Prophet SAW also described them as being relatively short. He also described him as being broad-chested. He also described him as having legs that are not straight. So, he's not walking in a straight way. He has basically deformed legs. So, these are all descriptions that are given of the Dajjal.

Women will follow Dajjal

It is also mentioned in a Hadith in Musnad Imam Ahmed, that that prophet SAW said, "The majority of people who follow the Dajjal will be from the Yahood, and also from the women". Now, why will the women follow the Dajjal? Because of the safety given at that time.

At that time there will be chaos. At that time there will be hunger and starvation. So, those who choose to follow the Dajjal, they will have that safety. So, it is possible that in that time frame, in that chaos, certain types of people will be attracted to the false promises of safety that the Dajjal gives.

Dajjal Will Not Enter Makkah or Medina

Now, we had mentioned that the Prophet said that, "The Dajjal will come from between Iraq and As-Sham. And he will go through every single city in the world, except of Makkah and Medina".

Now, we've already mentioned that the word used in the Hadith is Kul-Lu, which in Arabic does not necessarily mean 'each and every' without exception. Typically, it can mean the majority. Unfortunately, English most of the translators when they translators they translated it as each and every City. The point is that, Dajjal will go through the majority of the large cities in the world, except of Makkah and Medina.

We learn from the Hadith that our Prophet SAW said, "He shall try to enter Makkah and Medina and he will be stopped at the gates of Makkah and Medina by the Angels". So, if you want to be safe from the dajjal one of the things that you can do is to flee to Makkah or Medina during that time frame.

In the Hadith in Sahih Muslim, our Prophet SAW said that, "The Dajjal will try to enter Medina and he shall be prevented from doing so. And then he shall cause the city of Medina to tremble three times like an earthquake". So, the Jinn and the Shayateen will stamp on the city and there will be the notion of the earthquake. So, people will think that Dajjal is causing the destruction of Medina.

So, the Prophet SAW said that, "The Munafiqun will flee Medina. And Medina will be left pure with believers". Only people to remain in Medina will be those who believe in the Hadith. It's the prediction of Prophet SAW that, when Medina will start shaking, and there's a man outside the door, claiming to be god; you have already been warned by the Prophet SAW to stay in Medina.

Therefore, the only people that will remain in Medina will be the ones who believe in the Prophet SAW. Our prophet SAW said, "Medina is like a furnace. It separates the chaff from the purity. it filters the filth from the pure". And, he said this Hadith in the context of the Dajjal.

So Dajjal will filter through Medina and this also explains, about the Mahdi, why many of his followers will be from Medina. Because Medina will be completely pure. The believers of Medina will stay there and they will go out when the Mahdi comes. That is when the people of Medina will exit, and they will fight under the banner of the Mahdi and on the side of Isa AS.

So, Dajjal will come to Makkah and Medina, and will be prevented from entering both the cities. But wherever he goes, he will gather more and more followers. And he will gain a very, very large army.

Now we also learn we also learn that that the Dajjal will go to Medina, this is a very interesting Hadith. It is very explicit hadith in Musnad Imam Ahmed. And it says that the Dajjal will go to one of the mountains outside of Medina after he has been denied entry by the Angels. And he will take his followers to one of the mountains outside of the Haram's boundary.

Then, the Hadith says that, the Dajjal shall point to the Masjid and he shall say, "Do you see that white house? That is the house of Ahmed". And he will call Prophet SAW Ahmed SAW and not Muhammad SAW.

Why is this so interesting? Because if you ever fly into Medina, and you are looking down from the airplane, you will see a massive white complex. Because Masjid Nabawi, it's all marbles; and you can see it for many miles. And you can see it from the mountain tops.

This massive white complex that the Hadith explicitly mentioned, that Dajjal will point to and will call it the white Masjid or the white house is what the very structure that we have of Masjid Nabawi today. And Masjid Nabawi did not look like this in the time of the Prophet SAW. And Allah knows best.

It is a very sturdy structure. It can last many hundreds of years. Because current structure of Masjid Nabawi might be that very structure from the hadith. And we hope that the Dajjal will not come in our lifetime. And Allah SWT knows best.

Wars between Dajjal and Mahdi

Now we also learn from the Hadith of the Mahdi that, "The forces of the Dajjal and the Muslims will be fighting multiple battles, and the Muslims will be able to protect themselves partially. But they'll never be able to destroy the army of the Dajjal". And this is not explicit, but it's inferred.

This is a very, very key point, that the Dajjal will not be victorious in every battle. But he will be protected as a person. He will not be killed, and most likely, he's going to be harmed by nobody other than Isa AS. And Allah knows best about Dajjal getting harmed.

So, the Dajjal and his army will fight multiple fights, not just one. Now, maybe, Allah SWT knows best, and again all of this is surmising, that it's not even going to be one Army, in one location. Rather, they will be the forces of two camps fighting at multiple locations.

So, the world will be divided into two camps, and not necessarily one physical Army. Two entities will be fighting. One for the dajjal and the other fighting for the truth and righteousness and Taqwa and Allah SWT and his Messenger SAW.

It is possible that, in some of the battles and the skirmishes, the Muslims will be victorious and in some they will not be victorious. And we know this from the

Hadith of the Mahdi. Because the Prophet SAW said that, "The Muslims are going to be fighting armies at different places. Until finally, they will hear the cry that the Dajjal has come out, and he's attacking your family". So, they're going to go back in fear, that they're going to see the Dajjal.

But they will find out that it is a false cry. Which means, during that time frame, people will begin to recognize that this is the end of times, and the smallest rumor would provoke theories of Dajjal. Then, there will come a time frame, where they're just waiting for the Dajjal, and it will indeed happen that the Muslim army with the Mahdi is fighting somewhere; and the news will come that the Dajjal has come where your families are.

So, they will rush back towards As-sham, only to discover that the dajjal has not yet come. Then Dajjal will come. And we don't know how long after this news of Dajjal coming; but eventually, the Mahdi will be leading Salat Al-Fajr in Damascus and Isa AS will then come down.

So, all of this will happen in the time of the Mahdi. The fighting of Dajjal. Now, Allah knows best, because all of this is kind of, sort of deriving. And it's very terrifying in light of what is happening in the world right now. This is an interpretation that the forces of good and the forces of evil will begin to demarcate before the coming of Dajjal and before the coming of the Mahdi.

Because, there are already wars going on, and there is no Dajjal. there's already fighting taking place and the Dajjal has not yet come. But the situation is being prepared for the coming of Dajjal. So, it appears that there will be skirmishes, major wars, and bloodshed.

In some Hadiths it is mentioned that 99% of people will die. Will that happen with Dajjal or before Dajjal, we do not know. The Prophet SAW said that, "There will be such a massive war that the bird that is flying above will fall down dead".

Now, it's not too far-fetched to read that it could be a nuclear war. As Einstein famously remarked, "I don't know what World War 3 will be fought with, but World War 4 will be fought with sticks and stones". A very profound statement. That World War 3 is going to be the end of civilization as we know it, because of too much nuclear power.

Everything, the technology and the infrastructure etc. will be destroyed and we will be back to sticks and stones. Parenthetically, this also goes to another issue. There are Hadiths about horses being used in the time of Dajjal. There are Hadiths about swords being used. Do we take them literally? Allah SWT knows best.

Both opinions are valid, and it is permissible to call a weapon a sword. And it is also not unfeasible, not unrealistic, to assume that towards the end of times all technology as we know it, will be gone. And the only way that we can imagine this to happen, is a real and true Armageddon. Where something like an apocalypse is happening.

What's going to happen after all the nuclear explosions, when this whole world goes to war the next time? May Allah protect us, from time when nuclear weapons are used everywhere. What is going to happen to civilization? It will all be gone. We will be back to sticks and stones. We will be back to lighting fires with rubbing things together. We are going to go back to that time frame.

So, it is not inconceivable at all, to interpret these Hadiths literally, that the Dajjal and his followers, and the Muslims and the Mahdi, will be literally fighting on horses and with swords. Because all of the modern weaponry will be gone. Similarly, it is also possible that all of this is metaphorical.

Period of Dajjal's Existence

Now, our Prophet SAW said that, "Dajjal shall live 40 amongst you". It is the famous Hadith. How much time frame are these 40? Prophet SAW said, "One of them will be like a year, one of them will be like a month, one of them will be like a week, and the rest will be like your regular days".

So, we can calculate that Dajjal's time period is going to be roughly 14 months. But again, remember the Hadith of the end of time are cryptic. So, what does it mean the first day will be like a year? Does it mean that it will actually be one year? If so, then the time frame of Dajjal would be roughly 14 months.

Or does it mean that time will appear to go slow? Does it mean that everything will just appear like that for a long-time frame? Allah knows best. And this is a Hadith in Sahih Muslim. And this hadith also shows us the status of Salah.

That when the Sahabah heard this hadith, the first thing they said was, "Ya Rasool Allah how do we pray in that day, that is a year?" They are so much into Salah that the first thing their minds ask is, "how are we going to pray?" And our Prophet SAW said, "You estimate it".

So, another interpretation of this hadith is that, there will be no sunlight for a year. So, it will appear that one full year is as if it's the day and night. That's why our Prophet SAW said that we should keep on estimating the times of Salah, even if we don't see the Sun and the Moon.

And the only way that they will be no sunlight all over the world, is once again if these weapons of mass destruction are used. But Allah SWT knows best. It is a very valid reasonable interpretation. That year will be an actual year of 365 days. But people will not be able to recognize them as day and night. Then slowly but surely, the smog will settle.

So, the next one will be like a month. Then, things will clear up a little more, then a week and then regular days. And Allah knows Best. But we learned from this Hadith that the Dajjal will be on this Earth for a time that is reasonable. It's not that much of a stretch, if we say it is 40 days that feel longer; or it is 14 months. That's not too long.

Now, the 40 days mean that he will be Dajjal for that time frame. This does not include the time in which he will grow up. As we said, he will grow up as a regular child. He might not even know that he's the dajjal, when he's growing up. As the Hadith mentioned, that his Dajjal shall appear when someone provokes him.

Which means, in Isfahan something's going to happen, and he's just going to go berserk and ballistic, and then realize that he has these powers of Jinns and Shayateen etc. that others don't have. Then he will take advantage of that and go from bad to worse. Declare himself the Maseeh, get his followers, eventually declare himself God.

Followers of Antichrist

Our Prophet SAW said in a Hadith, that is in Musnad Imam Ahmed, that, "Most of his followers will be from the Yahood".

Now, what are the beliefs of Bani Israel about the Messiah? And why is our Prophet SAW saying that the majority of the followers of Dajjal will be from that group? Well, in Jewish eschatology about the term Maseeh specifically; They do have this Aqidah. It refers to a future king from the line of David AS.

So, mainstream Jewish belief is that, there will be a person from the line of David AS, from his descendants, who would be a king. And he will be anointed with holy oil. And he will bring in that Messianic age. And will bring in the end of times.

So, the Maseeh in their Aqidah is called The King. Because for them, the Maseeh is a political figure, and not a religious reformer. For them Maseeh is the one of power and politics. So, in Jewish traditions Maseeh is a King, who will bring about the restoration of the status of the Israelites, and reconstruct the temple of Israel.

So, they do believe in the Messiah, as a political figure and who will bring back the kingdom of Dawood AS. This has been Aqidah of ancient, medieval, and even some modern Jewish movements. That is why, when the

Messiah Isa AS came, and he began preaching to the Bani Israel. And he claimed that he was the Maseeh; the Yahood did not care about it.

They did not want a spiritual reformer. They wanted a Maseeh who is a king. So, when they found out that this person is not a king, they went and complained to the Roman Emperor. And they said, we have a man who is claiming to be the king of the Israelites.

Now, did Isa AS claim to be a king? No. He claimed to be the Maseeh. But to them Maseeh is a king. And they said to Roman Emperor that he is political agitator. Romans would not have cared, if they knew that Jesus AS was a religious reformer. But they did worry, that he's claiming to be a king. Because they want to avoid political a turmoil.

Now, Musa ibn Maymun or Maimonides is the single greatest theologian of Jewish law and Jewish theology. And he is only one that in all of their history, that they considered to be the greatest Jewish mind. He was an Arab. He spoke Arabic more fluent than any other language. He wrote in Arabic.

And there is a theory that, for a period of his life he was a Muslim. Because he studied in a madrasah. He memorized portions of the Quran. He studied Fiqh and Aqedah, in the Islamic tradition.

And one explanation for this could be that, because back in those days, all universities were run by Muslims. If you go to university in US, then you will have to take American history, political science etc. These are the required courses. You cannot graduate in this country, without taking these courses.

Well, once upon a time, if you wanted to go to any University and study engineering or medicine or Optics, you would have to study Fiqh, basics of sharia, Tafseer of Quran. This is exactly what needed to be done.

Now, He is called the chief Rabbi. He was the greatest Rabbi in the history of Judaism. He codified Jewish law. He is the first and most important Jewish figure to write a book of Aqidah, the book of theology. And he summarized it in 13 points. He called it the 13 principles of Iman.

Why did he summarize the Aqidah? Because he studied the Aqidah from the Muslims, and he wanted the same for the Jewish faith to have. So Jewish Aqidah, is actually coming from the philosophy of Ibn Rushed and others.

So, Musa ibn Maymun or Maimonides wrote a book called the 13 principles of Faith. Each of the 13 principals begins with the phrase, "I believe in this". In the 12th principle of these 13 principles is that, "I believe with full faith in the coming of the Maseeh. And even though he delays, with all that delay, I eagerly await his arrival. Everyday anticipating his arrival".

This is in the Aqidah of Maimonides. Which is the Standard Aqidah of the Jewish people, up until our times. This is the Aqidah that the Yahood would memorize, that they still believed to this day.

Now there has been a massive revival in the Orthodox Jew; and the Orthodox movement has swelled in ranks. And the reasons is because the modernist watered down the religion so much that there was nothing left. It was not a religion anymore. So, the people started to go back to an actual religion, that is orthodox.

Orthodox are the hardcore followers of Jewish faith. One of the strands of Orthodox is the Hasidic. Hasidic have a very strong and passionate belief about the coming of the Messiah. That it is very imminent. That it is just about to appear. And they believe that the more pious they are, the more quickly the Messiah will come. Hasidic are the most Masonic of the Orthodox.

Now with in Hasidic, the most prominent stand is called the Chabad movement. Chabad movement in particular, is the most Masonic. So much so, that one of the greatest Jewish figures of our times, who is an American, born in Russia, migrated to US, after fall of Germany, died in 1994. His name was Menachem Mendel Schneerson.

His followers began to claim that he was the Maseeh. That is how imminent it is. Still to this day, some of his followers believe that the Rabi did not die. That he is still alive in hiding. So, belief in Maseeh is common amongst the Yahood.

Therefore, do you think it is surprising that, when towards the end of times, somebody with power comes and claims to be the Messiah, and he is from that background; that lots of these people will then accept that claim? It makes sense. Now we understand, why our Prophet SAW said that many of his followers will be from Bani Israel.

Now Prophet SAW did not say that "Many of Bani Israel will follow Dajjal", but rather he said, "many of Dajjals followers will be from Bani Israel". Meaning, not all of the members of Bani Israel will be following Dajjal. They will also have amongst them who will distinguish Dajjal as being a Kafir.

Many of the Jews will recognize truth and falsehood. But from those who choose to follow Dajjal, many will be from that background.

End of Dajjal

Now, towards the end of times, when the big Armageddon battle takes place, and there shall be Dajjal on one side and Isa AS on the other. In that final Armageddon, Isa AS will kill Dajjal. And then all of the followers of Dajjal will disperse, running for their lives. Many of them will try to save themselves by hiding.

And the Hadith mention. This Hadith is in Sahih Muslim and there is a version of it in Sahih Bukhari. The Hadith mentions that, at that time frame, the creation will side with the supporters of Isa AS.

Because there will be Christians who will support Isa AS and believe in him. So, they will have become Muslims. And there'll be Yahood as well, who will choose to be with the truth. As Hadith don't mention that all of Yahood will follow Dajjal. The majority of Dajjals followers will be from there. But number of them will be with Isa AS.

So, the Hadith mentions that every tree, and every rock wall say to the believer, "Come here, there is that person behind. He is hiding". So that there is no use to hide anymore. Because the creation of Allah SWT will publicly humiliate them. Except for the tree of Gharqad. That is a tree that will be quiet and not side with the Muslims.

Now the Hadith mention where Dajjal will be killed and it is explicit in Sahih Muslim. The Prophet SAW said, "Isa will kill Dajjal at the gate of Lud". And it is verified that both Muslim and the other side, claim this. So, there seems to be no Ikhtilaf, that Lud is essentially where the modern airport is of Israel. So, it does appear to be that, that is the place. It does seem to be the case and Allah knows best.

Return of Bani Israel to the Holy Land

Now, this leads us to a very interesting issue. Now, we have mentioned that the Christian belief is very similar to our beliefs. Especially the Evangelicals and Baptist.

That Jesus is the Messiah and he shall come back towards the end of times. That there should be a false Messiah, the Antichrist. And the Christ and Antichrist will fight. And that Christ will win over the Antichrist in the great Armageddon. In this rough outline, we are the same.

Of course, there are many differences. Of them is that this will only happen when the Bani Israel are gathered in the Holy Land. We do not have this as an explicit mention. But they do. This is the belief of Evangelicals, that Jesus will only come back, when all of the Bani Israel are gathered in the holy land.

Therefore, because they want to see their lord and savior, they are eager to bring the Bani Israel into the Holy Land. And it is because of this, that some of the most hardcore Zionists are not people of the Jewish faith. They are Evangelicals. Because it is there Aqidah that with the return of the Jews to the promised land, their savior will come back. So, they went to expedite that.

Now, they believe that when the Savior comes, the first things he's going to do is to get rid of those who didn't believe in him. Primarily, according to their Aqidah, the people who tried to kill him, or actually succeeded. Because they believe they succeeded.

Now, this group wants to support the Bani Israel to go to this land, with the Aqidah that they will all be destroyed in that land. You understand this? They are ardent Zionist. And they have no love for the people whom they're helping. On the contrary, their Aqidah is that the very people they're helping, will be destroyed.

Wallaahi, this is mind boggling. Now, how can the other group accept their aid, knowing that this group wants us dead? And one of the Rabbi was actually asked this question, that, "How can you accept help from people who think that helping you will eventually cause you to be killed? The very people who want to get rid of you, are helping you, with belief that, you will be gotten rid of".

The Rabbi smiled and said, "Well that's their belief. If they want to throw money and power at us, we will not reject it. What they believe in is not going to happen". In a nutshell, what he meant is that, "If they're irrational enough to believe it, that's their business. We're going to still accept their power and help".

So, we have to understand this point as Muslims. Also, these beliefs are not held by Catholics. Every Christian group is different. The Mormons have their own beliefs. The Seventh-Day Adventists are totally different in this regard.

Wars in the of End Times

So, we have mentioned warfare with the Mahdi, when we discussed the concept of Dajjal, we discussed it with coming down of Isa AS to a great extent. It is interspersed and referenced many times. Now we will discuss this sign of Judgment Day in detail. And that is the wars, or the fighting, or the Armageddon, or the great battle, that will take place before the end of times.

So, this is referenced a number of times. There are many traditions that mention warfare towards the end of times. And the fact of the matter is that, these traditions although numerous, they are cryptic as usual. Because we don't have a chronology. We don't know if all of these Hadiths are talking about one war, or many small wars, or wars that will go on over many decades or many centuries.

We don't have any clarity. It's simply predictions of Judgment Day. And there are some hadiths that simply say, "Of the signs of Judgment Day is Kital". That there will be warfare, and the Prophet SAW predicted that, "You will have days of Haraj, Haraj, Haraj". The Sahaba said, "What is Haraj?" The Prophet SAW said, "bloodshed". So, there are predictions of lots of wars.

Now, is this hadith pointing to civil war at the time of the Sahaba and the wars throughout Islamic history, where the Muslims are fighting? Or are we talking about only one timeframe? This is where there are no clear answers. And Allah SWT knows best.

So, we will be looking at Ijtihad of other Scholars in terms of piecing things together. Then we will try to work through a chronology to build an understanding of all of the hadiths on this topic. And Allah SWT knows best.

Now, an understating is that, these hadiths predict a continuation of wars from the time of the Sahaba until the Great War. The first category of wars is that, there are a number of a Hadiths that mention civil war between the Muslims towards the end of times. A massive war that will take place between the Muslims.

The second category is that, there's a series of hadiths, that mention a big war between Muslims and an ally and a non-muslim. So, Muslims with one group of non-Muslims will fight another group of non-Muslims. And then the third category, that there are hadiths about the big war. In Arabic, it is called Al Malhama Tul Kubra. This is a prophetic term. Al Malhama means the disaster or the catastrophe or the bloodshed.

This is the equivalent of the Christian concept of the Armageddon. So, there are a number of hadiths that mention a civil war. That is not the Armageddon. That's before the Armageddon. Then there are hadiths that mentioned a big war, but not quite as big as **the** big war. So, these will be big wars, but not **the** big war. This is all Ijtehad, because some Ulema have merged them all together.

Then there are hadiths that mention the big war. And of course, the big war, is Al Malhama, that is between ISA AS and the Dajjal. That is **the** final battle, that will take place. After that, there might not be any more wars. That it might be the end of all wars. And then other things will happen after that. And Allah SWT knows best.

In summary, what we are talking about is, first, a series of continual small battles will take place. The Prophet SAW predicted that, "Once the sword is unsheathed from my Ummah, it will never be put back". This is a generic hadith. The Muslims will be continually fighting trivial battles. From the time of the Sahaba, major battles have taken place, such as Battle of Siffin and Battle of camel.

In continuation, throughout Islamic history, Muslims have been fighting one another. It is happening today as well, that Muslims are fighting one another. This is standard. It is going to happen. Then there will come a time, where there will be major wars between the Muslims.

Then, there will come a time when there will be a major war between a team of Muslim and non-muslim on one side, and one other non-muslim on the other. Now, whether this is going to be before or after the big major war between Muslims; we don't know. And then it will conclude with the big war Al Malham Tul Kubra.

Civil War Between Muslims

So, let us discuss some of those traditions and get a clearer understanding of what this notion is. We begin with the famous hadith, that is authentic. Abdullah bin Rawaha RA said, "We were with the Prophet SAW. And we complained to him, how poor we were. And that we didn't even have clothes to wear".

So, the Prophet SAW said, "Rejoice! don't worry about that. for I am not worried that you will live in poverty. Wallaahi, this Ummah will be in continual good; until Allah Subhana WA Ta'ala opens up the lands of the Persians and the lands of the Romans and the lands of Yemen".

So, in Makkah, the Prophet SAW predicted that we will conquer the Persian Empire and that happened. That we will conquer the Byzantine Empire and that happened. That we will conquer Yemen and all of that happened.

Then the Prophet SAW said, "You will become three armies". Now, this is the Ummah. This is the Civil Wars we talked about between the Muslims. And the Prophet SAW said, "An army will be in As-Sham. An army will be in Iraq. And an army will be in Yemen. And wealth will be so much, that a man will be given 100 dinars and he will think that it is nothing".

Now 100 dinars from Prophet SAW's time will be our five thousand or ten thousand dollars. It's a large amount, but not an extremely large. But this is not going to have any value in the end of times as per eh hadith. In other words, wealth will be so much, that a good amount of wealth would be considered utterly trivial.

Ibn Rawaha RA said, "Ya Rasool Allah, when that happens, which of these three armies should I be with?" The Prophet SAW said, "I tell you to be in the army of As-Sham. Because it is the chosen of Allah SWT's people. And it is where the Qiyamah will take place".

Now, another hadith that was mentioned with the concept of the Mahdi, that is in the six books and it is an authentic hadith. Our Prophet SAW said that, "Three sons of Khalifa will fight amongst them for your treasures".

So, there will be a treasure belonging to the Ummah and three sons of a Khalifa, or three princes will be fighting. All of them are from a royal family. So, these are within the Ummah. This is the internal civil war, that we mentioned before, at end of times. And none of them will be victorious. All three are going to fail.

Then, the black flags will come from Khurasan, and then the Mahdi. So, there will be an internal civil war. This hadith shows us that the Mahdi will come at a time when the Muslim Ummah itself is internally fighting and the Mahdi will unify the Ummah from within.

The Ummah will need a leader. The Ummah will need somebody they can trust. Someone whose integrity is beyond doubt. The person that they will look up to and the person they will unanimously go behind, is none other than the Mahdi. With the Mahdi that civil war will be finished.

So, this is a very clear indication that there shall be a time of massive internal civil war between the Ummah. And when you look at what is happening now, with the internal superpowers. And that there are already massive wars going on. Muslims are dividing amongst themselves. Each one of them doing its own and Muslims are being harmed in the process.

So, we should be very terrified looking at what is happening in the world and looking at these hadiths about the end of times. And Allah SWT knows best. So, this is the issue of the internal war.

War that 1% Survive

Now, of the other wars that are predicted; one hadith mentions that one of the Tabi'un was in Kufa. And Kufa was the land of Ibn Masud RA. Ibn Masud RA established his madrasah in Kufa. The greatest Sahabi of Kufa was Ibn Masud RA. And he died in Kufa as well.

So, Ibn Masud RA was in Kufa and one of the Tabi'un, his name was Hussain ibn Jabir; he said, "One day it was very cloudy and a dark dust storm came in the daytime and it blocked the Sun. And it seemed very terrifying. So, a man came shouting to the Masjid, 'O ibn Masum, the day of judgment is coming'".

Looking at what is happening, he became terrified. He's running to Ibn Masud RA saying that the Qiyamah is coming. Ibn Masud RA then stood up amongst the people. The people are looking to him for comfort and for wisdom. The people are terrified. They're gathered in the Masjid. Ibn Masud RA stood up and he said, "The Qiyamah will not come until"; and then he gave a series of predictions.

Now, whenever a Sahabi, a companion, mentions something about Ilm Al Ghaib, automatically what he says, becomes a hadith. This is a rule. Whenever a Sahabi says something about the knowledge of the unseen, it becomes a Hadith.

If a Sahabi speaks of Jannah; if a Sahabi speaks of Judgment Day; that on the day of judgement such and such will happen; if a Sahabi speaks about the signs of the Judgment Day; automatically that statement gets upgraded to a Hadith. Because how could a Sahabi speak about the unseen, unless he had heard it from the Prophet SAW.

Now, if a Sahabi says something is Haram or halal, this remains the opinion of a Sahabi. Because that is Ijtehad. And the Sahaba's opinions did differ about Haram and Halal on things that were not clear in the Hadith. Just as all of the great scholars did. But there Ijtehad has a high level. But it doesn't become a Hadith of the Sunnah.

But when a Sahabi speaks about Allah SWT, his names and attributes, the signs of judgment day, it automatically gets upgraded to a hadith. Such hadith begins as a statement of Ibn Masud RA, as this hadith does. Then in the middle, Ibn Masud RA says, "And then the Prophet SAW said". So, we even proved the rule through this hadith that he's narrating what the Prophet SAW.

Now the Hadith does not begin in the middle, when he subconsciously says, "And then the Prophet SAW said". It becomes Hadith from the beginning. Because it talks about the knowledge of the unseen.

So, Ibn Maud RA stood up. And this hadith is in Sahih Muslim and it's a long hadith. Ibn Masud said, "The Qiyamah is not going to come until you see these signs". And given these signs have not come, this cannot be the Qiyamah.

He said, "People will not be able to divide their inheritance". This means that massacres and death will be so profound, that a person will have no family left. And, "people will not be happy over Ghanima or war booty". Once again, it means there are no people left to distribute it amongst.

Then he pointed towards Syria. He is in Iraq, at the time of saying this Hadith. And he said, "And an enemy will gather forces against the Muslims there. And the Muslims will gather forces against them". A man in the audience said, "By enemy, do you mean the Romans?" Ibn Masud RA said, "Yes". Now the Romans here refers to European civilization and the Christian empires.

We have already extrapolated the concept of Romans to the modern nations that look up to that Empire as being there theological and their intellectual ancestors. So, the term Romans can apply to the majority of civilization, the superpowers of our times. This is interesting because these are predictions that we are now seeing taking place

Then he says, "At that time, there will be severe fighting. The Muslims will send a battalion to fight to death and they will not return. they will die. they will fight until night. neither side will be victorious over the other. on the second day, the Muslims will send another battalion, and they will fight to death, and they will not return victorious. On the third day, the same thing will happen".

So, for three days, Muslims will be going in and it is going to be a massacre, after massacre. Nobody will remain alive from the first batches that go.

And he said, "Then on the fourth day, Allah SWT will grant victory to the Muslims, and the enemy will be defeated". So, there will be four days of battle, somewhere in Syria. Now this is not the great Armageddon. It is the precursor to the Armageddon. This is a massive war, that will take place before the Armageddon.

Now the hadith goes on, and this is from the statement that, "This will be a battle, the likes of which have never seen before". This is very terrifying. In human history, no battle has taken place that is more terrifying and more severe than that battle, that will take place towards the end of times.

And then, Ibn Masud said, and this is so powerful. That the Prophet SAW, "So much so, that a bird that will fly over them, will fall down dead". Now, no matter how many people are killed by the swords on this land, it will not affect a bird in the heavens. What will affect a bird in the heavens? Definitely not swords. I hope you get the point. Something will happen that a bird in the heavens will be flying over, and it will come down dead.

Then the hadith goes on, "Out of a family of 100, 99 will perish, and one will survive". The attrition rate in this war, will be 99%. What war in human history has had 99 percent deaths? None. The victory is given to the 1%.

This is when, the Prophet SAW said, "How can anyone be happy over Ghanima or any inheritance being divided". In other words, may Allah SWT protect all of us; but if somebody were to give you a million dollars, but you have no family. Wallaahi, no sane person will choose that. Family is worth more than this whole dunya.

So, the Prophet SAW is saying, that how can anybody be happy, when he gets all the Ghanima and 99% of his family are dead. That he has nobody left. No parents, no children, nothing is left. So, this war will destroy 99% of those fighting in it.

Now, while they are finishing the battle, collecting the Ghanima, and recovering; "They will hear that there's a bigger calamity than this That someone will shout out that Dajjal has come, where your families have been left behind".

So, in that state, tired, bruised and bleeding; but given their families are being attacked, they will rush back to that land. But they will discover that it was a lie. And in one hadith, it is mentioned that, "They will send their ten best horsemen to go verify that news". Meaning, the ten fastest horsemen.

And then, the Prophet SAW said, "I know their names and the names of their forefathers and the colors of their horses. And they will be the best horsemen on the face of this earth". Now does this mean that we will go back to horses and swords? If there is that type of war, in all likelihood we will.

If there is that type of war where nuclear weapons are used by every side, then we will go back to those days when there was no electricity. Or, it is possible that when the Prophet SAW is saying horse, he means a vehicle. This is also possible. It's not too much of a stretch. And Allah SWT knows best.

Now this hadith does not mention the Mahdi being part of this war. But other hadiths mention that the Mahdi will be there, when the news comes for the first time, that the Dajjal has come out. So, it appears that this big war, that is being referenced, is a war that the Mahdi will participate in. Even though he's not mentioned in this particular Hadith.

So, it is a war between Romans and between the Muslims. Now, many Scholars have said that this hadith is a reference to the Armageddon. it could be true. Because it is not clear whether Armageddon is one battle or is it a series of battles? If it's only one battle, then in all likelihood, that will be Dajjal and Isa Ibn Maryam AS. But if it is a series of major battles, then it makes sense that this hadith, in fact, is one of those big battles of the Armageddon. Allah SWT knows best.

War of the One third

The next hadith, which is a very cryptic one. It is authentic hadith and it is the hadith in Sahih Muslim. Abu Huraira RA narrated that, "The judgment will not come until Ar-Rum will come out to fight you at a place called Amaq or Dabiq. and the best of the people of earth, from the city of Medina will leave Medina and fight against them. When they are getting ready for war, the Romans will say to the Muslims, 'leave us with the group amongst you, who have forsaken their religion. We want to fight them'. And the Muslims will say, 'We will never abandon our brethren'."

So, the battle will rage on and, "One third of the Muslims will retreat, out of cowardice and Allah SWT will never forgive them". When the battle gets tough, they will flee. And the Prophet SAW said, "They will never be forgiven".

Then hadith says, "And one third will be killed and they will be the best of the Shuhada". So, they stood their ground, and they died martyrs and they will be the best of Shuhada. Then hadith says, "And One third will conquer. They will win and they will not be tested".

This may be the test of the grave, or may be the test of the Akhira. Allah SWT will bless them and they will not be tested. Then hadith says, "That one third will then conquer Constantinople".

Hadith Continues, "When they will be dividing their Ghanima, after they've hung their swords on the trees to be oiled, then they will hear Shaitaan cry out, that the Dajjal has appeared amongst their children. Thinking it to be true, they will march to fight Dajjal. But they will find it to be a lie. They will reach Balad As-Sham and when they have lined up to pray Fajr, that is when Isa Ibn Maryam AS will come down; after the dajjal has actually come. And he will then lead the Muslims in war. And when the Dajjal sees Isa Ibn Maryam, he will melt like salt is dissolved in water".

And the Prophet SAW said, "If he were to be left in that state, he would die. But Isa will kill him and the people will see the blood of Dajjal on the weapon of Isa".

Now again, this hadith is very cryptic. It mentions many things. First and foremost, it also reiterates the previous concept of a massive war between the Romans and the Muslims. Now, in this hadith, it mentions only one-third will die. Whereas the previous hadith mentions 99% will die.

So, it appears there will be multiple battles, not just one. In some of them 99% will die and in some of them one-third will die. This hadith mentions that, this army will conquer Constantinople. Whereas, the previous Hadith does not mention that. So maybe, there are multiple wars going on in the world. And that the Dajjal's announcement will take place in all of them.

Shaitaan is going to frighten the Muslims that Dajjal is here. They're going to be expecting Dajjal, because they're seeing the Hadiths taking place. So, Shaitaan will use it as a tactic. So, maybe multiple groups will run back to Balad As-sham and there they will be with the Mahdi. And the Mahdi will then be leading them in Salah. And Dajjal will actually have come at that point in time. Then Isa AS will come down as we had mentioned.

Now for the cryptic phrase, where Ar-Rum are going to ask Muslims to hand over their brethren and the Muslims will say that they are not going to hand over their brethren. What is all of this? This is very interesting, and Allah knows best. It appears that there will be a large group of converts from Bilad Ar-Rum to the land of Islam. And they will be fighting on the side of the Mahdi and the Muslims.

And the Bilad Ar-Rum are going to view them as being traitors, from their perspective. So, they will say, 'First we want to deal with these traitors, because they betrayed us and our values'. And the Muslims will say, 'They're not your comrades. They're our comrades. We will never abandon our brethren for you'. This hadith is in Muslim.

Now, in context of Isa AS, in Surah Nisa, Allah SWT mentions, and it's not explicit, but Allah SWT is talking about Isa AS; that, "He is a sign of judgment and there is no person of the Ahl Al Kitab, except that they will believe in him before he dies". This has been interpreted by our Ulema to mean, this is a reference to when the righteous Christians see Isa AS, when he comes back, they will believe in him.

It's really profound and Insha'Allah, it indicates that there will be massive conversion. So much so that the Balad Ar-Rum remnants are angry, and irritated. Now, this also shows that these a hadith are not anti-Semitic or anti-Western. It is good versus evil. You will find people of all ethnicities on the side of good and you will find people of all the ethnicities on the side of evil as well.

Malhama at Bilad As-Sham

Another hadith that mentions all of these as well, is that the Prophet SAW said, "The fortress of Muslims on the day of the Malhama, will be at Ghouta". This is where the Armageddon is mentioned. Ghouta which is a city near Damascus. One of the best cities in As-Sham. This hadith is an Abu Dawood. It is an authentic Hadith.

Three things are mentioned here that is Ghouta, Damishq, and Bilad As-Sham. Ghouta is a small city, that is still inhabited to this day. When the Prophet SAW said this hadith, all three were the heartland of the Christian Byzantine Empire. These were not the lands that belonged to Islam. But the Prophet SAW predicted that these places will be a part of the Ummah. And that when the great Malhama takes place, the fortress, the base, the camp of the believers will be in the city of Ghouta in Bilad AS-Sham.

Of course, the concept of Balad As-Sham is mentioned many times in the hadiths. The Prophet SAW said in an authentic Hadith that, "When the Fitan occurs, Iman will be in Balad AS-Sham".

Now, from these series of incidents, what can we extract from all of this? First and foremost, realize that Bilad As-Sham doesn't just mean Syria. Bilad As-Sham in classical Arabic, pre-Sykes-Picot agreement of 1917, and before the partition of the Muslim Ummah and the

Ottoman Empire; Bilad As-Sham was essentially Syria, Jordan, Palestine and Israel. So, Palestine is also Bilad As-Sham from hadiths perspective.

Also, it shows us that towards the very end of all of these trials, the Muslims will be united and they will be fighting outsiders. They will be fighting non-Muslims. And the people from other lands will come to Medina, because they have to fight on the side of the truth.

It is also very clear that these wars are taking place with the Mahdi being in command. With the Mahdi in command, there is no civil. So, this is a war between the Mahdi and the believers on one side, and the unbelievers on the other side. It also shows as I said that in all likely scenario, we're talking about multiple Wars. And Allah SWT knows best.

The Mahdi himself will be going region to region. In one battle, one-third will die. In another battle, 99% will die. Allah SWT knows best. Again, we don't know. We're trying to putt all of these together. And the fact that the bird is mentioned, shows that this isn't your typical war. That chemical or nuclear seems very likely in these types of hadiths.

Khilafa in Ard-Al- Muqaddas

Now another hadith and a very interesting narration, that goes back to Abdullah bin Hawala RA. He has a number of interesting narrations about judgement day. Abdullah bin Hawala RA says that the Prophet SAW said, "Oh bin Hawala when you see Khilafa having been descended to Ard-Al- Muqaddas then know that the Zalazil and the Fitan and the Balayah are coming".

Ard-Al- Muqaddas here means Jerusalem. Meaning, the great wars are going to happen. And the Prophet SAW said that, "And know that Qiyamah is closer to mankind than my hand is to you or to your head". And Prophet SAW's hand was on Ibn Hawala RA's chest.

Now, this hadith tells us, that there shall be a Khilafa, but not based in Makkah or Medina. Not based in Iraq like the Abbasids. Not based in Damishq like the Umayyads. But rather based in Ard-Al- Muqaddas. Now, in all likelihood this is the Mahdi. Some scholars have said that may be this is before the Mahdi. But most like this is the Mahdi.

Because the Ummah has never been united since the time of Uthman RA and Ali RA. And it is not going to get united again, until the Mahdi comes. Also, our Prophet SAW predicted that, "The Khilafa will come back towards the end of times. There shall be a Khilafa upon the prophetic methodology". In all likelihood this is

Mahdi. And Allah knows whether this Ijtihad is correct or not.

But in all likelihood, it seems to be none other than the Mahdi himself. And the Prophet SAW is telling Ibn Hawala RA, "When the Maddie comes, judgment is going to come tomorrow". And that's very true. When the Mahdi comes, the judgement is going to be coming immediately after that.

Re-Conquest of Constantinople

Now, another issue that is explicitly mentioned is the conquest of Constantinople. Of course, Constantinople is named after the Roman Emperor Constantine. So, Constantine basically made the city his capital, and Constantinople became the bastion of human civilization for almost a millennium. This was the city and the land. There was no competition with any other civilization, up until the coming of Islam. For a thousand years almost, Constantinople was the cradle of civilization.

And amazingly our Prophet SAW predicted that Constantinople will be ours again. We are coming so many centuries later, we don't even think about this. One of the most significant episodes in recorded human history is the conquest of Constantinople. This is something that we just take for granted. Most of us have no clue. But in reality, it was the most cataclysmic, the most seismic disruption that happened in medieval history. Because it essentially signified the end of the Roman Empire. And the conquest of Islam over the Byzantine and Roman Empire. And then it was renamed Istanbul.

And Subhan Allah, the Hagia Sophia is an amazing testament to human mind. This is a building that was built before the birth of our Prophet SAW. And our Prophet SAW predicted the conquest of Constantinople.

But there's a problem that there are other a hadith that mentioned this conquest will take place towards the end of times, when the Dajjal is around the corner, and when the Mahdi is around. So, this creates a conflict in our understanding. What does that mean? Allah knows best. There is no explicit, clear, unambiguous answer.

The only thing that can be said is that, that land will revert to being controlled by a group that is not sympathetic to Islam. Even if they call themselves Muslims. And Allah knows best. Maybe things are going to change in that land may Allah SWT protect all Muslims. And there will be a reconquest of Istanbul.

Also, the Hadiths mention that that reconquest will take place miraculously without any blood being shed. That was not the case in the first conquest. It was a bloody war that lasted many months. It was the standard war and many people died in it. That's not what the hadith predicted.

And you cannot enact a hadith. Alhamdulillah Sultan Fateh conquered it, but that's not what the hadith predicted.

Now this is a hadith in which Abdullah Ibn Amr ibn A's RA said that, "You will fight Constantinople three times". Now, does he mean the city of Constantinople;

or does Constantinople indicate the Roman Empire or Europeans? Either can be there.

So, "You will fight Constantinople three times. The first time is that you will do well but you will not succeed. The second time you will enter into a Sulah with Constantinople. So much so that Masjids will be built inside Constantinople".

Now, this is really inexplicable, because Masjids did not exist in Constantinople up until 1453. And now there are only masjids in Constantinople. But does this is what it seems to be referencing. So, again Allah knows best, if the conquest of Sultan Fateh is what the hadith is calling the Sulah.

Then he says, "Then you will return for a third time and you will conquer it with the takbir. You will say Allahu Akbar and it will be conquered". And the Prophet SAW said that, "One-third of Constantinople will be destroyed, and one-third will burn down, and one-third will be divided amongst you".

Now this hadith seems to indicate a final conquest of Constantinople. And this is mentioned in another hadith, which the majority of scholars hadn't have interpreted to mean Constantinople. Now this hadith is authentic and is in Sahih Muslim. These two hadith seem to add some concept.

The hadith is as follows; the Prophet SAW asked the Sahaba, "Have you heard of a city, half of which is in the water and half of it in the land?" And in another narration, Prophet SAW Asked, "Have you heard of the city part of it is in the water and part of it is in the land?"

The vast majority of our commentators have said that this is Constantinople. Because Constantinople essentially divides Asia from Europe. So, the majority of our Ulema, including Ibn Kathir RA say that the Prophet SAW is describing Constantinople. And the Sahaba said, "Yes we have".

Then, the Prophet SAW said, "The Qiyamah will not happen until 70 thousand of the Bani Ishaq will conquer it. And when they come to it, the Bani Ishaq will not fight with swords. Nor will they fight will arrows. Rather, they will say La Ilaha Ill Allah Allahu Akbar, and one of the sides will fall down. Then they will say La Ilaha Ill Allah Allahu Akbar, and another side will fall down. Then they will say La Ilaha Ill Allah Allahu Akbar, and then they will say it again, until all four sides will be fallen down. And then they will enter the city and begin to distribute its Ghanima. And while they are distributing its Ghanima, the Shaitaan will call that verily Dajjal has come out to your family. And they will leave everything and return to their family".

Now, we've heard the similar hadith before. But now we have an added detail that 70,000 of the Bani Ishaq will conquer Constantinople. So, it is plausible, very reasonable, to say that the armies of the Mahdi will be fighting at multiple places in this world, and some of the fighting will be more severe than others, and one of the very end of this series of battles will be the Battle of the conquest of Constantinople.

But in this battle, there will be no war, there will be no blood, there will be no swords. it will be a miracle given to them. The people in that battle will come and find the walled gates. They will realize they cannot fight the people of the city. But they will know this hadith. As the Prophet SAW is telling them to use this tactic. And they believe in the hadith so they will use this tactic.

And they will conquer the city without any bloodshed. Then false news of Dajjal's arrival will come. They will flee back to As-sham. Then when they're in As-sham, Dajjal will actually come. And then, they will be fighting him a few times. And then Isa AS will come.

Now who are the Bani Ishaq? Some Ulema have said that this is a reference to the Romans. That's what the Arabs would call them. This is one interpretation. In another interpretation, it means the converts of the Yahood. Now, the term Bani Ishaq never occurs in any other hadith. And Allah knows best.

Now, 70,000 in Arabic does not mean exact census 70,000. it is a broad figure. It is a figure of speech. Like in English we'd say, "I called you a dozen times". But it doesn't have to be a dozen. In Arabic, seventy is the generic. So, the Prophet SAW is saying that there will be seventy thousand converts. It could mean a hundred thousand.

This not as minor amount. And they are fighting on the side of the Muslims. And it is at their hands, the hands of the converts, that Constantinople will be conquered. Not at the hands of the born Muslims. It will be those who are pure. Those that have chosen to fight with the truth. Allah SWT will bless them. That when they say the Takbir, and their Takbir will cause the walls of the city to fall down.

Now, this is the standard interpretation. But a number of scholars say this hadith doesn't apply to Constantinople. Another group of scholars says, this hadith is a reference to Venice. And we say maybe. Allah knows best. Because this hadith doesn't give a name. However, there are other hadiths that mention Constantinople by name. There are no hadiths that mentions Venice by name. So, Allah knows best.

Romans with 80 Flags

Now, there's one set of hadith left, that during one of these series of wars, or maybe before all of this begins, because we don't know the chronology. It is mentioned that towards the end of times, the Muslims and the Romans will form an alliance against a third party.

This Hadith is very atypical from the other hadiths. Because all the other hadith mentioned the Romans on one side and the Muslims on the other side. So, it is an opinion and Allah know best, that these hadiths apply at the beginning of the Armageddon. Or at the beginning of all the wars.

Things are going to happen, where Muslims and Romans will ally with one another, and then that Alliance will be destroyed only to get worse and worse, until the Mahdi and Dajjal and Isa AS come. And Allah knows best. And during this timeframe, people would convert from the Roman side to the Muslim side. Now these hadiths of this alliance and treaty are authentic hadiths.

This hadith is in Abu Dawood that, Awf bin Malik Al-Ashjai RA said that, "I visited the Prophet SAW during the Battle of Tabuk. When he was in the Battle of Tabuk. And his tent was made out of leather. I sat in front of the tent. The Prophet SAW gave me permission to come".

So, he came in and the Prophet SAW said to Awf RA, "Oh Awf, count six things before judgment will happen". The Prophet SAW gave him prediction. number one, "My death". Awf RA said, "As soon as I heard that, I was shocked and saddened".

Subhan Allah, the Prophet SAW not being amongst us, is something we don't notice, as we were born that way. For the Sahaba they could not imagine a world without the Prophet SAW. The Prophet SAW, he's emphasizing the first sign of Judgment Day is the death of the Prophet SAW. That's the beginning of all the signs.

Number two, he said, "then the conquest of Bait al-Maqdis". This conquest of Bait al-Maqdis happened in Abu Bakr RA's time. Subhan Allah, the last day of Abu Bakr RA's Khilafa was the conquest of Bait al-Maqdis. The first day of Umar RA's Khilafa, he received the news of the conquest.

Now, when the Prophet SAW said this, it was impossible to even think of Bait al-Maqdis being in Muslim lands. It is one of the biggest miracles of the truth of Islam. That our Prophet SAW predicted these things, and they took place within a year after his death.

If you really understand history at that time, this was impossible to conceive of, that this small group of Muslims in Medina, who have not yet even conquered Makkah; and they're going to go conquer Bilad As-Sham, and Bilad Ar-Rum and Bilad Al-Faris. Yet within a year, that took place. One of the most unexpected historical turns for Western historians is the rise of Islam.

It is inexplicable. They cannot explain it. That how could a group assorted Bedouins, from their perspective, came and disrupted human civilization and destroy the Sassanid Empire, carved out the Byzantine Empire, and created a civilization that was even more glorious than the both of those previous ones combined. They don't understand how that happened.

So, for us, our Prophet SAW said number two, it will be the conquest of Jerusalem. Number three, "A plague that will come amongst you, and destroy your children, and your wealth, and property, and it will purify your good deeds". Our scholars say, this is the plague of Amwas in the eighteenth year of the Hijra. There was a massive plague in the time of Umar Ibn Al-Khattab RA. it was the worst plague of early Islam.

Number four, "Wealth will be distributed amongst you. So much that if a person is given 100 dinars, he would not be happy". The Sahaba were very poor. One dinar was a big deal, and a hundred dinars was a fortune to them. And we're now at a time when a hundred dinars is of small value.

Number five, "There will be a fitna, a trial, that will not leave any of your houses, except that it will touch it".

Our Scholars say, in all likelihood, this is the fitna of the Sahaba. That every single household was affected. Battle of Siffin, Camel, that first civil war that took place. Others say, this might yet be another fitna that will happen later on.

Then number six, "There will be a treaty between you and the Romans. Then they will betray you and march against you with 80 banners. Under each of which will be 12,000 troops". In other words, a hundred thousand people. This hadith is in Ibn Maja.

Another hadith mentions that, "You will form a treaty with the Romans, and you will fight an enemy common to both of you. Then you will be victorious and as you are returning back, one of the Romans will raise the cross on a mount and say, 'This has caused us victory'. Then, a Muslim will get angry and destroyed that cross, and say, 'Allah has caused us victory'. And war will break out and the Romans will break their truce. And then they will march against you with 80 Banners".

So, these are only two hadiths about this prediction that there will be a third enemy. Who is that third enemy? Allah SWT knows best. But it's neither the Muslims nor the Europeans. But once that enemy has been gotten rid of, then the Romans will essentially break their treaty with the Muslims. Because of this minor skirmish between two people.

But the Romans will take that as an excuse to destroy the treaty and they will then attack Muslims. They will march against Muslims with 80 banners. That's a major war. This is another prediction of a great Armageddon that will take place. And Allah SWT knows best.

Now, is this the Armageddon or is it one of them? Again, it's all cryptic. It can also be said that the final battle between Dajjal and Isa AS will be an easy battle and not a difficult one. That the Muslims will not die in mass, in that battle. Victory in that battle will be a gift from Allah SWT to the believers. The hadiths are not explicit. But it can be derived.

We derive this, because when the Dajjal sees Isa AS, he will scream aloud and flee away, and dissolve, and Isa AS will kill him. With Dajjal being killed, and his followers seeing Dajjal being killed, they will all start to scatter. That's when the creation will say, "come and kill the person behind me".

So, the interpretation is that the final battle between Dajjal and Isa AS is not the Malhama. The Malhama is the battle before it. Which is this one, with the Romans and 80 flags on one side, and the Muslims on the other. As for the actual final battle, it will be a gift because there will be no resistance from the other side. So, these are the multiple interpretations of Malhama. Allah SWT knows best.

Christian Understanding of Armageddon

Now what is the Christian understanding of the Armageddon? The word Armageddon is a Greek word. That itself comes from a Hebrew cognate and a Hebrew origin word 'Har Megiddo'. Har means a hilltop and Megiddo is the name of an ancient city that now falls in the Land of Israel. And this city is close to the city of Nazareth. And it is north of Jerusalem.

This city, even in pre biblical times, even in ancient times, was a city that was inhabited by the ancient Canaanites. It has been inhabited for last 7,000 years and is one of the ancient cities of the world. The Bible mentions the city of Megiddo multiple times. There are cryptic references in the Book of Revelations, that there will be this massive war.

The Book of Revelations is a book in the Bible, in which there are predictions for the future. So, for the Christians the Book of Revelations has predictions of the Beast 666, and the Antichrist. It's very cryptic. That's why even many Christians don't read. it's not an easy text to understand. So, there are cryptic references in the Book of Revelations, to the big battle at Har Megiddo.

Hence the term Armageddon comes from Har Megiddo. And there are a number of interpretations of modern-day Christians with regards to these statements. Many Christians, this is the default amongst the non-Protestants. Many of them reject this as tales. Again, as Muslims we should learn Christianity, if we want to be involved in Dawah. Not all Christians are the same. Just like not all Muslims are the same. Many Christians don't consider the Bible to be the word of God.

This is the default in America, that the majority of Christians do not take the Bible literally. So, if the book of Revelation says something, it's of no value. However, some strands of Christians take the Bible literally. And in particular, Evangelicals and the Baptist are well known for this.

So, they have a very particular belief in the second coming of Jesus, and in the resurrection of the dead, and in the rapture, and in the Armageddon. Baptists, in particular are associated with the strand called pre millennialism. Premillennialism believes that the second coming of Jesus Christ will be in two stages.

That Jesus will come, and there will be a seven-year period of tribulation. The beginning of that will be something called a rapture. What is the rapture? The rapture for this strand of Christianity, is that when Jesus comes down, Christians will rise up to meet him in heaven. That's the rapture. They will meet him Midway.

And they believe that for seven years, there will be this battle between the forces of good and evil. The Antichrist will come. Incidentally, seven years is also in Islamic literature.

There's going to be forces between the Antichrist and the righteous people. Then Jesus AS will come down after seven years and defeat the Antichrist. Then there will be permanent peace on this earth. And then there will be judgment after that. Some Christian sects believe that when Jesus comes again for the second time, that is judgment right there and then. There is no heaven and hell.

So, the seventh-day Adventists, that's what they believe. That there is no heaven and hell for them. They believe that the coming of Jesus is in itself heaven and hell. The point being, we need to understand Evangelical support for modern politics, in light of the belief of the rapture and the belief of the coming of Christ and Antichrist.

Over 80 percent of Evangelicals say that the creation of Israel in 1948 is a partial fulfillment of the Biblical prophecy. And it is signaling the coming of Jesus Christ. That is why Jerusalem as the capital of Israel is all a part of the Biblical prophecy as well. It is all a part of what they believe will happen before the coming of Jesus Christ and before the rapture.

Now, Armageddon from their perspective, who's going to be on the other side? Muslims and Palestinians. So why would they have any love for that group of people? Think about it. It is because they have a theology that is clouding their humanity.

They're not looking at them as breathing, living individuals anymore. They're looking at the second coming of Jesus. They're looking at Jesus coming back. They want to expedite that process. From their perspective, who is the Antichrist? They call our Prophet SAW that. Nauzubillah! Nauzubillah! But we need to understand that this theology impact politics.

These are realities that impacts policies that impacts us. So, we need to understand that our beliefs, which are different from Christian beliefs. We believe many of the Romans will convert and side with the truth. But they don't believe that. They believe all Muslims will be in the army of the Antichrist. That's their Aqidah. So why should they have any sympathy for us?

That's why we need to educate ourselves and educate them, about this important topic. And clarify that our beliefs are different. We also believe in the coming of Jesus, and we will be on the side of Jesus AS. And they will have to decide to be on the side of truth or be with the side of falsehood.

Ya'juj and Ma'juj

Now, we move on to the next of the major signs and that is the subject of Ya'juj and Ma'juj. And the issue of Ya'juj and Ma'juj is actually for our modern times, is one of the most problematic of the signs of judgement day. It has caused many of our youth to question and doubt.

Some people have actually left Islam because they could not comprehend this concept. We have to be honest and not pretend as if this problem with our youth doesn't exist. We are dealing with the crisis of people leaving our faith. Our own children, our own young men and women.

The reasons are that we are not answering some of these issues, that they bring. And we dismiss them. I myself have discussed many of these issues with these types of people, and one of them, is Ya'juj and Ma'juj. So, we have to be very clear and think critically as we look at our tradition.

So, who are Ya'juj and Ma'juj and what does the Quran and Sunnah say about them? The issue of Ya'juj and Ma'juj is something that doesn't just occur in the hadith. It is explicit in the Quran. So, Allah SWT mentions Ya'juj and Ma'juj in the Quran. It is also found in many Hadiths as well. But in the Quran, it is mentioned in in two specific verses.

Surah Al-Kahf

The first of them is Surah Al-Kahf. At the very end of Surah Al-Kahf, Allah Subhana wa Ta'ala mentions the subject of the story of Dhul Qarnayn. and Allah Subhana WA Ta'ala says, "We gave him power in this world. And we allowed him a path everywhere". So, he went to the easternmost part of the world and he went to the westernmost part of the world.

There are stories mentioned in the Quran about Dhul Qarnayn, that he was a just king. He thanked Allah Subhana wa Ta'ala. He found people of all different types and persuasions. Then the final group of people, that is mentioned, when he came to essentially a valley, where there were two mountain slopes coming.

Allah SWTS says in the Quran, "He found a group of people. They did not understand Dhul Qarnayn, and Dhul Qarnayn did not understand them". In other words, this was a civilization that had no middle ground. In the old days, before internet apps that translate speech easily, how did people used to translate for one another? There were intermediaries, who had traveled to both lands. That there will be a person who spoke both Latin and Arabic, for example.

So, Dhul Qarnayn went to such a faraway land, that the language of those people and the language of Dhul Qarnayn had no middle ground. So, Allah SAW is mentioning, this is a far-flung civilization from where Dhul Qarnayn came. So, how did they communicate, when there was no other way? They communicated with Signs.

Just as a tourist, in a different land, who doesn't speak their language and is forced to communicate with his hands. And Mashallah, you can communicate so much with your hands. So, they are communicating with their symbols and with their gestures.

So, they say to Dhul Qarnayn, and this is the first mention of Ya'juj and Ma'juj. They say, "This group of people Ya'juj and Ma'juj, they are wreaking havoc in this world. So, Dhul Qarnayn, you are a mighty king, you are a powerful person. We will give you something and in return, you build a wall to protect us from those people. Dhul Qarnayn, you are clearly a man of intellect and power. You have a civilization that we do not have. You have strength that we do not have. So, we want you to do something to protect us".

So Dhul Qarnayn has gone to the furthermost regions of the world, and there is a group of people even beyond that region, that is called Ya'juj and Ma'juj. And this civilization is saying, 'We want protection. We'll pay you to build this barrier between us and them'.

So Dhul Qarnayn says, "I don't need your money. I have plenty. Rather, I understand these people are evil". So

Dhul Qarnayn sympathize with this nation, against Ya'juj and Ma'juj. So, Dhul Qarnayn said, "I'll help you. But I need from you your strength and manual power". So, he knows what he has to do. He has a plan. But he needs the people to execute it.

So, Allah SWT then mentions that, they took big bellows of furnace and iron and copper; and they used these bellows of the furnaces and a massive scale and they made a special type of a massive iron barrier.

Allah SWT mentions, "Neither could they climb over the wall. Nor could they come underneath it. Nor could they bore a hole between it". So, it is an effective barrier. Dhul Qarnayn when he saw what he had done, he said, "This is from Allah". That Allah SWT has blessed him. That, 'This is not from me. It is from Allah Subhana WA Ta'ala'.

Then Allah SWT is speaking that, "But this wall is temporary. When the command of Allah comes, then this wall will be of no use. And on that day, these groups will be like waves just intermixing amongst one another. And the trumpet will be blown".

So, this is the first mention of Ya'juj and Ma'juj, and it deals with the wall that was built by Dhul Qarnayn.

Surah Al-Anbiya

The next mention of Ya'juj and Ma'juj is in Surah Al-Anbiya verses number 92 to 97. Where Allah Subhana WA Ta'ala mentions in the Quran regarding Judgment Day, "Until finally, Ya'juj and Ma'juj will be allowed out; and they are going to be pouring down from every single slope. From every mountain, they're going to be coming. And judgement will now be asunder and will now be well close".

So Ya'juj and Ma'juj are right before Judgment Day. This is very clear in the Quran. In both Surat Al-Kahf and Surah Al-Anbiya Allah SWT mentions that "The inevitable hour is coming, once Ya'juj and Ma'juj are released, right before Judgment Day".

Dhul Qarnayn

Now, who is Dhul Qarnayn? Dhul Qarnayn is an enigmatic figure. And most of our medieval commentators thought that; and especially the most famous translator of the Quran of the previous century, Abdullah Yousuf Ali. Abdullah Yousuf Ali, in his translation and his commentary, he mentions that Dhul Qarnayn is Alexander the Great. And this thought kind of spread amongst the masses even though it is incorrect.

Dhul Qarnayn being Alexander the Great is hundred percent wrong for many reasons. Most obvious reason is that, Alexander the Great was not a believer in Allah SWT. He was a pagan. He worshiped the idols. Allah SWT praises Dhul Qarnayn as being a worshipper of Allah SWT. Allah SWT praises Dhul Qarnayn as being a righteous person. And Allah SWT never praises paganism. Allah SWT never praises someone in this manner.

Allah Azza Wajal mentions Dhul Qarnayn says, "This is from Allah". So, Alexander being Dhul Qarnayn is really impossible. Some modern commentators have said that, it is the Persian king Cyrus. King Cyrus who ruled from around 600 to 530 BC. We're talking about 2600 years ago about the Persian king Cyrus. And they say, Cyrus is a candidate because he ruled over perhaps one of the largest empires the world has ever seen.

There have been many massive empires. Alexander the Great, probably did rule over the largest empire at the time. But it was temporary. Alexander's empire fizzled out with his death. With Cyrus, firstly there are a number of things that don't match up. Secondly, once again Cyrus was a clear-cut pagan.

Now, there is a third theory that some are sympathetic to. But these are just theories at the end of the day. It's the opinion of some modern scholars that, if Dhul Qarnayn were a historic figure, because it is always possible that Dhul Qarnayn existed prior to the recorded history. Because recorded history begins around 4000 years ago. Before that, we don't really have records. Before that is just unknown. Perhaps Dhul Qarnayn is of that timeframe. And SWT Allah knows best.

So, we know almost all of the massive empires and the great kings that have existed in last 4000 years. If Dhul Qarnayn was one of the kings of this era, then we should know about him. In terms of recorded history, humanity would have known of these types of great kings, who have conquered large swaths of the earth.

So, another candidate, that many are sympathetic to is the Persian Emperor Darius. The Persian Emperor Darius ruled from 550 to 486 BC. Darius ruled over most of the known world at that time. Most of what we now call Asia Minor, the Caucasus, the Balkans, Central Asia, Egypt, and North Africa. He had a massive empire. He himself traveled to the furthest east and the farthest west.

He led expeditions in in his entire kingdom and he fought against the Egyptians, he fought against the Chinese. And what is interesting about Darius is that unlike Cyrus and definitely unlike Alexander, Darius was a monotheist. In contrast to the people before him and after him, we know from the books of history that Darius was an ardent monotheist. He was a strict believer in one God.

He was beloved to his people. He had the reputation of being a just king. There are records of Darius' inscriptions in which he is saying, "I am The King Darius whom God has bestowed power to". In other words, he is saying that, 'God has blessed me with this power'.

it is very rare to find an ancient king, who basically thanks God for his kingdom. For instance, Firon claimed to be a god, instead of thanking Allah SWT. It is very rare to find an ancient king, who says, 'I am a king, but the one above is the one who made me the king. He's the one who gave this to me'. Also, there's a very enigmatic inscription of Darius in which he is depicted as having two horns as well. Now, some say, Darius was a Zoroastrian. So, Allah SWT knows best.

It is also possible that, Dhul Qarnayn could be somebody in recorded history, whom we don't know. But that seems to be a difficult scenario. So, Allah SW knows best.

Now, Dhul Qarnayn is called Dhul Qarnayn according to our tradition, either because he had two streaks of white hair, or because he wore a helmet with two horns, or because he went to the east and the West. So, this is the notion of Dhul Qarnayn.

Hadiths about Ya'juj and Ma'juj

Now, we discussed what the Quran tells us about Ya'juj and Ma'juj. In the Quran, we don't have much detail about them. Other than that, they seem to be a race of savages. They seem to be race that is barbaric. They are killing, looting and plundering neighboring places. And Dhul Qarnayn, who had never met them before, is sympathetic to the victims. He builds a wall to protect these strangers from Ya'juj and Ma'juj.

So, what does the hadiths say about Ya'juj and Ma'juj? There are numerous Hadiths about Ya'juj and Ma'juj. In fact, in the six books of hadiths, there are around a dozen narrations of Ya'juj and Ma'juj. Bukhari and Muslim have around seven Hadiths on Ya'juj and Ma'juj. So, it is mentioned in the most authentic books.

Of these hadiths, is the hadith in Sahih Muslim, where our Prophet SAW said, "Ten are the major signs of Judgment Day". And he mentions Ya'juj and Ma'juj amongst them. We have mentioned this hadith earlier in the book as well. So, number six on this list mentions Ya'juj and Ma'juj. So, he mentions Ya'juj and Ma'juj as being one of the ten major Signs.

In another hadith, that is in Sahih Bukhari and in Sahih Muslim. The Prophet SAW says that, the Prophet SAW recited the initial verses of Surah Hajj in the Quran. Where Allah SWT mentions that, "This is Judgment Day.

That O mankind fear your Lord. For indeed the earthquake of Judgment Day is something to be terrified. On that day, you will see that the mother will neglect her breastfeeding child. And people will walk around as if they are drunk, but they are not drunk. But the punishment of Allah is severe".

The Prophet SAW quoted this Ayah, and then he said that, "When will this happen? When will people be so terrified? When Allah will announce to the Angels, to take the people of Jahannam to Jahannam. And from every 1000, 999 will go to Jahannam".

The Sahabah said, "Ya Rasool Allah, with those odds, how can we be safe?" Because if out of every 1000, 999 will go to Jahannam, what is the statistical chance of the Sahabah to go to Heaven. And the Prophet SAW said, "I give you good news. For every one of you, there will be a thousand of Ya'juj and Ma'juj".

So, this hadith is saying that the quantity of Ya'juj and Ma'juj is astronomical. Beyond what we can even comprehend.

The hadith is in Musnad Imam Ahmed, that the Prophet SAW said that, "You complain that there is no enemy". Because some of the younger Sahabah are wanting to have a fight. So, the Prophet SAW says, "But you shall continue fighting. There will always be Kital, once the fitna begins. And there will always be fighting **until** Ya'juj and Ma'juj come".

So, hadith is explicit that fighting will continue until Ya'juj and Ma'juj. Then the Prophet SAW described them. That, "They shall have faces, that are flat. They shall have eyes that are narrow. They shall have hair that is yellowish. And they shall descend from every single plane".

Now important to note is that, we shall fight until Ya'juj and Ma'juj. He didn't say, 'You will fight Ya'juj and Ma'juj'. What we learn here is that we will not fight Ya'juj and Ma'juj. Ya'juj and Ma'juj are not something we can fight. They We cannot fight and win against Ya'juj and Ma'juj.

Fighting will continue **until** Ya'juj and Ma'juj come. Which also means, after Ya'juj and Ma'juj come, there is no fighting. Ya'juj and Ma'juj is the final frontier, after which there will be no Fitan. This also shows that Ya'juj and Ma'juj will be of the very, very, very, last Fitan to take place, because there will be no more Fitan for the Muslims.

The Prophet SAW said as well, in another hadith from Sahih Bukhari that, "I swear by him, in whose hands is my soul. You shall continue to perform Hajj and Umrah; and you will continue to cultivate and plant trees; even after Ya'juj and Ma'juj". So, in Sahih Bukhari, we learn another interesting fact, that Ya'juj and Ma'juj is not the end of the Ummah. The purpose of this hadith is to tell us that the Ummah of Muslims will not be destroyed by an external enemy.

This is a prediction, that has been true throughout all of history, and it will continue to be true. So, the Prophet SAW in this Hadith is giving glad tidings to the Shahab when they were worried about the Quraysh. He is telling them not to worry. That not only will the Muslims survive, but they will do Hajj and Umrah. Meaning we'll retain our religion. And we will cultivate; meaning retain our dunya. This will continue, even after Ya'juj and Ma'juj. Even Ya'juj and Ma'juj are not the end of Muslims. So, this is another interesting thing that we derived.

In another hadith, that is in Bukhari and Muslim, it says that the Prophet SAW was with some of his wives, and he was agitated. He was concerned and worried. He put his finger and his thumb together in a circle. And he said that, "Woe to the Arabs". And this means Muslims, because at that time all the Muslims were Arabs.

So, he said, "Woe to the Arabs, from an evil that has now come very close". Umama Salama RA asked, "What is this evil?" He said, "Today a hole of this size has been opened up from the wall of Ya'juj and Ma'juj". And he described the size of the hole with the hand gesture.

Now, this hadith is the highest level of authenticity for us.

Umama Salama RA said, "Ya Rasool Allah, will we be destroyed and there are still righteous people amongst us? Will piety not save us?" And our Prophet SAW said, "Yes, even if there are still pious people, but if filth is prevalent everywhere, the piety of some individuals will not protect you. It might protect them on Judgment Day".

In fact, their piety will protect them on Judgment Day. But societies will not be protected. When corruption and evil and fitna and licentiousness and nudity and Fahisha is rampant everywhere, the piety of a few folks will not prevent the Azab of Allah SWT from coming. If you understand this hadith, then you should make sure you are at least pious.

So, this hadith tells us that, the wall of Ya'juj and Ma'juj has a hole the size of a small circle in the lifetime of the Prophet SAW.

Now, a hadith in Tirmidhi, in which Abu Hurairah RA narrates that, "Every single day Ya'juj and Ma'juj try to dig out. And every day they are met with an Angel. And the Angel tells them, "Enough for today. Go back". So, they go back. And the Next day, when they come back, they find all of the work that they had done, has gone back to nothing. They have to start from the beginning again".

And the prophet SAW said that, this will continue, until on the final day, the Angel mentions the famous phrase, "Insha Allah come back tomorrow", after asking them to go back; then when they will come back the next day, they will find that the work of yesterday is still there. They still are carved in. So now, they start from where they left off and then they will break through.

So, this is a hadith that mentions that Ya'juj and Ma'juj are carving every day and that every single day they get to a place, until the Angel turns them back.

In another hadith in Sahih Muslim, we learn that after Dajjal is killed, Isa AS will congratulate his followers and give consolation to his followers. And within that time frame, or very shortly after that, Allah SWT will inspire Isa AS that a new group has come. That, "Creations of mine have come. No one can fight them. So, take my servants and go to mount Tur. And protect them over there".

Then Allah ST will send Ya'juj and Ma'juj out. So, Isa AS and the Muslims will not see them. They will be protected in the caves of Mount Tur. Now, in this hadith we learn that Ya'juj and Ma'juj are so dangerous, so evil, that Allah SWT Himself says that, "Nobody can fight them".

Interestingly enough, this army has just fought Dajjal and his army. And they have won over the Dajjal. And they are told that, "You cannot fight Ya'juj and Ma'juj". In fact, Allah SWT protects them from even seeing Ya'juj and Ma'juj. They just flee by the command of Allah SWT, before Ya'juj and Ma'juj come. They find protection in the caves that Allah tells them to find protection in, before Ya'juj and Ma'juj come.

And they will remain in those caves for a time period that Allah Subhana Wa Ta'ala knows best. In fact, in one narration, Prophet SAW mentions that, "Isa AS and his followers will seek refuge in a cave, for so long, that the head of a Ram will be more precious to them than 100 gold dinars".

Now, the head of a Ram is almost useless. It has no meat. It has nothing you can benefit from. You throw it to the side. But they will be in the cave for so long, that a head will be more precious to them than a fortune. As they have nothing to eat and drink. Until, finally when they will notice something. Now, the hadith doesn't mention what it is that they will notice. But they will try to decide amongst themselves, on who can volunteer and go and see what is going on outside the cave.

So, a man will volunteer. He will be considered the best of them. And he will resign himself to die the death of a Shaheed. He's given up. And he has accepted that he's going to die the death a Shahid. But he will come out only to see that the world is full of corpses of Ya'juj and Ma'juj. Then, he will call out the people and they will come out, and they will see not a single hand span of the earth except that it is piled with Ya'juj and Ma'juj.

The world will stench. There will be a stench that they cannot bear from bodies of Ya'juj and Ma'juj. So, they will desperately plea to Allah Subhana WA Ta'ala. And Allah SWT will send a rain that will cleanse the earth. A cleansing that it has never had before.

In another narration, Allah will bring a special type of bird that will pick up their bodies and take them away. So, we have the removement of the corpses. Then we have a special rain that will wash away the remnants as well. So, this is another tradition from Sunnah Tirmidhi.

We also have in Musnad Imam Ahmed the phrase which is also in other books as well, that, Allah SWT will send Ya'juj and Ma'juj, and they will descend from every single plane. And they will pass by At-Tabariya. They will drink from At-Tabariya, which is a massive lake. And by the time the last of them passes by, there will be no water in the lake of At-Tabariya. The last batch will say, "There used to be water over here".

Isa AS and his followers will remain trapped in a cave, until the head of a lamb is more precious than 100 gold coins. Then they will make dua to Allah SWT to save them from Ya'juj and Ma'juj. So, Allah SWT will send a disease against them. Ya'juj and Ma'juj would not be killed with the sword. Allah SWT will send a disease against them, that will attack their necks and they will die the death of one person.

When one of them dies, all of them will die. It is a simultaneous death. The death of one person. These billions of people they will die instantaneously. Then this man will come out, terrified and scared. He will find that Ya'juj and Ma'juj are already dead. Then Isa AS will come out. They will find not a single space to stand except the bodies will be rotting there. So, Isa AS will make dua again.

So, Allah SWT will send birds with the necks of Bakhtari camels. The Bakhtari camels have u-shaped necks. There will be massive birds with massive beaks. They will take away the bodies of Ya'juj and Ma'juj.

Yet another narration says that, "Ya'juj and Ma'juj will conquer everybody in this earth. They will kill everyone". Now, who will they kill? Clearly not the followers of Isa AS. These will be the remnants of the army of Dajjal, who fled and were not caught. Any human beings, that have not embraced Allah SWT and believed in Isa AS at this point in time; these will now be destroyed by Ya'juj and Ma'juj.

So Ya'juj and Ma'juj will conquer the world. They will get to At-Tur, where Isa AS is. And in one narration, they will get to the Jabal of Quds. And they will find nobody to conquer. They've conquered everybody. So, one of them will say, "We have conquered the inhabitants of this world. Let us conquer the habitants of the heavens".

Then, they will throw an arrow towards the heavens and Allah SWT will cause the arrow to come back full of blood. In another narration, they will waive their spears towards the heavens and Allah SWT will cause their spears to come back with blood. And they will say, "We have now conquered those in the heavens". Then Isa AS will make the dua, and then they will be destroyed.

Now, this lake Tabariya, most of our commentators mention that this is the Lake Tiberias and this is also called by the Christians, the famous Sea of Galilee. The Sea of Galilee, it is a massive lake. It has massive amounts of water. It has fed the crops and the people for three thousand years.

What group is Ya'juj and Ma'juj that in one generation, that lake which has given mankind water for three thousand years will be gone. Think about that how much will this group drink. The Sea of Galilee is like a mini ocean. You can barely see the end. All of this water will be gone in one group.

Also, what type of enemy is this that the people of Isa cannot physically even fight them. Because they fought

Dajjal and his people. They are not even seeing them. The man who's going to go see them, is thinking he's going to die just by looking at them. He's already made up his mind.

So, we also have in a number of traditions as well, what demonstrates their quantity. The Prophet SAW said that, "The Muslims will use the weapons and the armor of Ya'juj and Ma'juj for many years to come".

In one hadith, in Musnad Imam Ahmed, the Prophet SAW said, "The beasts of the earth will grow fat and feed themselves for many years, from Ya'juj and Ma'juj". So, the corpses will be so much that Ya'juj and Ma'juj will fertilize the earth. And from this fertilization there shall be a time of great opulence.

In terms of food, perhaps the most opulent time in the history of mankind will take place. Where our Prophet SAW said, "One pomegranate will feed an entire tribe. One leg of lamb will be enough for a large group of people".

In other words, things are going to change. It either means that Small quantities will suffice large group of people; or maybe there will be changes to size of single food items. Maybe the pomegranate will be of a massive size.

In Sunnah Ibn Majah, the Prophet SAW said, "When you see Ya'juj and Ma'juj, then expect the hour to come, just like the pregnant lady at the end of her labor is just waiting for the cry, and she surprises the family when she goes into the pangs of labor". In other words, Qiyamah is at that very end stage. So, when you see Ya'juj and Ma'juj, at that time frame Qiyamah is just waiting to happen.

classical Understanding of Ya'juj and Ma'juj

Now, what do our classical scholars say about Ya'juj and Ma'juj? Firstly, is the term Arabic or is it non-Arabic? Our scholars, some of them have said that the term is Arabic, and it comes from word Ajjah. Ajjah means to kindle fire or when the fire spurns outwards.

However, in some opinion, it is not sound to read in Arabic meanings of proper nouns, that are found in the Quran and Sunnah. Because Arabic language is not what was spoken between Dhul Qarnayn and the people affected by Ya'juj and Ma'juj. And those people called the raiding tribes Ya'juj and Ma'juj. So, it was another language. And Ya'juj and Ma'juj might have completely different meaning in that language.

Ya'juj and Ma'juj is a classical noun that has very little to do with Arabic. Also, the term Ya'juj and Ma'juj is found in pre-Islamic literature. Term Gog and Magog is found in pre-Islamic literature. It is mentioned the old testament and in the new testament.

The Book of Revelations mentions the Gog and Magog and the release of Gog and Magog. That Gog and Magog are going to gather for the battle. The Book of Revelations predates Islam. There is references to Gog and Magog, that they're going to gather for their great battle as well.

The Midrash also mentions Gog and Magog. What is the Midrash? The Midrash is Tafseer literature and the commentary on the Torah for the Jews. The Midrash consists of legends and fables that go back many centuries before Islam. You have the Babylonian Midrash.

So, the Midrash is pre-Islamic Jewish exegesis. it is Tafseer literature that is ancient. It's not the Torah. It is the commentary of the Torah, that the ancient sages, the Rabbis of the past commented on. The Midrash say about Gog and Magog, that there will be a forerunner to the Messiah. Now, there actually are some segments of Judaism, that believe in two types of Messiah. The minor Messiah and the major Messiah.

So, they say that there will be a forerunner to the real Messiah. And this forerunner will defeat Israel's enemies. When they say Israel, they don't mean the country. They mean Bani Israel. So, they say that, this Jewish messianic precursor, the minor Messiah, will defeat Israel's enemies Gog and Magog. And then the real Messiah will come, and then judgment will take place. Then the righteous will be rewarded.

Meaning, with Jannah; if that's their reward. Now, this is interesting, because this is Midrashic literature and it mentions two figures. It mentions Gog and Magog and it mentions Judgment Day; all in the same paragraph.

Allah SWT knows best, but we have the Mahdi, we have the Messiah, we have Gog and Magog, we have day of Qiyamah; all in the same paragraph as well.

So, Gog and Magog are mentioned in the Quran and Sunnah. It is mentioned in the old and New Testament. It is mentioned in Midrashic literature. How have our historians understood Gog and Magog? Ibn Kathir RA mentions that, "Ya'juj and Ma'juj are from the children of Adam". So, they are Bani Adam. They are not an alien species. They are flesh and blood like us.

Some of our early historians have said, and this is not in Quran and sunnah; they say that, "Ya'juj and Ma'juj goes back to Japheth Ibn Noah. Now this motif is biblical and it is found in the Tabi'un. It's not in the Quran and Sunnah. We find in our early history that Noah AS had three sons, Sam, Ham and Japheth.

From Sam, we get the sematic people. That is the Arab and the Hebrew race. And according to this interpretation, Persians and the Romans. In fact, as per this theory, middle Easterner are Caucasians. If you're Arab or Desi you're technically Caucasian. Ham is the father of African peoples. And Japheth is the father of the Atraaks, the Slavs, Russians, the Mongolians, and the Ya'juj and Ma'juj.

Given this motif is from the Old Testament and it is not found in the Quran and Sunnah, but in where early Islamic historical traditions; it something that is not necessarily widely accepted.

There is a genre called Israeliat, where some of our earliest scholars they would study the Midrash and they would study the Jewish folklore. At that time the Jewish folklore was considered to be a civilization worthy of admiration and respect. So, they would take this and then speak it in Arabic to the masses. But the people would think that this is a part of Islamic traditions. Even though it is coming from the Midrash.

But, Ibn Kathir RA says that, "they are the children of Japhet". And this is the standard interpretation of the majority of our medieval scholars. The fact that Ya'juj and Ma'juj are Bani Adam seems pretty clear from our tradition. Bani Adam is human beings. We learned this from a number of evidences.

Of them is the famous hadith in Bukhari, where Allah SWT says to Adam AS, "O Adam, take the people of hell to hell. And he shall take his children". And that's when the 999 out of 1000 will go hell comes in. So, the fact that his children includes Ya'juj and Ma'juj, shows that they are Bani Adam.

Now we have some unauthentic interpretations. That, once Adam AS had a wet dream, and his fluid fell on the earth, and that earth sprouted forth, and it became Ya'juj and Ma'juj. We also find in another unauthentic interpretations that Ya'juj and Ma'juj are Bani Adam but not Bani Hawwa.

Now, standard interpretation of Ya'juj and Ma'juj is the following. This is found in Ibn Kathir RA, it is in the Tafseer literature, of al-Samarqandi. Basically, this is the conventional interpretation for our classical and Middle Ages of Islam. Ever since the beginning of writing Tafseer, up until pre modernity.

The notion is that Ya'juj and Ma'juj are a strange exotic tribe in the nether regions of the world. That have been trapped by Dhul Qarnayn thousands of years ago. And they're still trapped to this day.

Location of Ya'juj and Ma'juj

Now, in perspective of our times of science and geography and modern civilization, we have some other interpretations. The first interpretation is that, there are places in the world that are undiscovered. That there is a race of people locked and not discovered.

Others have said, we need to reinterpret Ya'juj and Ma'juj metaphorically. And this interpretation is newfangled. We do not find it in pre modernity. This is a very modern interpretation. It only begins in the 60s and it has now become very common. It says that, the Dajjal and Ya'juj and Ma'juj are symbolic. It's not an entity. That Dajjal is globalization and Ya'juj and Ma'juj are the superpowers of today.

This interpretation is not valid, as the problem comes that hadiths give the concept of Dajjal, they also tell us a lot of details about Dajjal. That can't be interpreted this way. These details mentioned are very vivid. The impression given that Dajjal will be killed by Isa AS in a battle, his blood will be on the spear, that it will be shown to everyone. And that the corpses of Ya'juj and Ma'juj will be piled up everywhere. These clearly indicate that they are not a metaphor.

A third interpretation is that, Ya'juj and Ma'juj are the Chinese race, and the great wall that was built by Dhul Qarnayn is the wall of China. Now this notion also is not valid. Of the problems of this interpretation is that we know exactly who built the Great Wall of China, and he wasn't a believer in Allah SWT. And the Great Wall was actually built to protect the Chinese people from within, not from without. And the Great Wall is not a barrier that is impenetrable. People go in and out of the wall all the time.

Another group say that, perhaps Ya'juj and Ma'juj are not on earth, but under earth. That's why the satellites haven't discovered them. This opinion is not valid because human beings cannot survive underground, with no Sun, and oxygen etc.

Now, there is no clear-cut answer to this conundrum of location of Ya'juj and Ma'juj. But Wallaahi, to struggle with the truth and to admit the struggle, is a safer position, than to invent something that is far-fetched and then pretend that it is answering the problems. The location of Ya'juj and Ma'juj should not be something that Muslims should concentrate on and leave it on to Allah SWT.

Now, another opinion suggests that seems plausible, is perhaps this notion of a living tribe of Ya'juj and Ma'juj is not correct. Because there is only one tradition that is in Tirmidhi. There is only one Isnad that mentions that Ya'juj and Ma'juj are digging on the wall every single day, and they're told to go back. All the other traditions don't mention a living Ya'juj and Ma'juj; other than the hadith in Buhari that the wall has been opened, and Prophet SAW uses hand gesture to signify size of hole.

As for the hadith of opening of the hole in the wall, in this case, it could be a metaphor that indeed Ya'juj and Ma'juj are now closer to us. The only tradition that mentions that Ya'juj and Ma'juj are alive right now and they are digging through every single day is a solitary narration in Tirmidhi. And in fact, some of the classical scholars have problematize this hadith. Amongst them is Ibn Kathir RA.

Ibn Kathir RA said that, this tradition seems to be a defect. That it is not coming from the Prophet SAW.

That it might be coming from the Isra'iliyyat. Because Abu Huraira RA also used to study with Ka'ab al-Ahbar, who was the son of a rabbi, and he would narrate Isra'iliyyat to Abu Huraira RA. And one of the students of Abu Huraira RA assumed it to be from the Prophet SAW. This is Ibn Kathir RA saying this.

So as per this interpretation, Ya'juj and Ma'juj is a group of people that will come towards the end of times and they will wreak havoc. So, they are not alive right now. And as for the wall of Dhul Qarnayn, they may be the biological ancestors of those that will come at the end of times. They were a tribe that had those characteristics and they were trapped. That did happen.

But as per this interpretation, we don't have to affirm that they are still trapped thousands of years later. Rather maybe they are descendants. May be people similar to them. That is why they are called Ya'juj and Ma'juj. And Allah SWT knows best.

There is another interpretation, which is very plausible, and is the most modern of all other interpretation. It says that, the wall that was built by Dhul Qarnayn was not a physical wall, but rather a barrier. That Dhul Qarnayn created a barrier, that somehow trapped Ya'juj and Ma'juj in an alternate dimension.

Just like Jinns have their own dimension that is different than our physical world. Or the world of the dead is different than ours. Same way, Ya'juj and Ma'juj are trapped in a world that is different and parallel existing to ours.

So, when Allah SWT, before the end of times, dissolves that barrier, they will start pouring from all directions. Just as the hadiths say. Otherwise, if it was a physical wall, and it goes down, they would still come out of just that one location.

Also, if it is a barrier between worlds and not a physical wall, that explains the Hadith that they try to dig through every day and the wall undoes the work. As a normal physical wall is incapable of regeneration.

That also, explains how a wall that is thousands of years old, is still existing without any maintenance. And lastly, it explains the Ayah of the Quran that says that the wall of Dhul Qarnayn is not something that can be climbed, or dug under, or dug through. Because it is not a physical barrier, it doesn't need maintenance. And as it is not like a wall that we can climb it or dig through or under it. Both of these things are also not possible.

This also explains how 100s of Billions of Ya'juj and Ma'juj, the population so large that 999 out of 1000 will be going to Jahannam is able to exist. Imagine the physical space needed to accommodate that many people.

Our world is already being called over populated by scientific community, by having just 7 billion people. Causing the shortage of food, global warming and greenhouse gasses etc. This would be a lot worse, if the population of Ya'juj and Ma'juj was also on our plane of existence. And Allah SWT knows best.

So, these are some of the common interpretations regarding location of Ya'juj and Ma'juj.

Why Not to Theorize on Predictions

So, we conclude by stating that Ya'juj and Ma'juj are a reality. We believe in them, because the Quran believes it and mentions it. And that these enigmatic descriptions should not cause us to doubt. Because strange things will happen towards the end of times. Don't base the validity of Islam on trying to understand Ya'juj and Ma'juj.

We base the validity of Islam on the Quran, on the beauty of Islam, on Tauheed, on La Ilaha Ill Allah, on the fact that it answers all the big questions of life. Islam comes with some things that may be beyond our comprehension. Such as Ya'juj and Ma'juj. We just have to leave it on to Allah SWT. And when it happens, all of these hadiths will fit into place. And we will get what was being referenced.

Why we are hesitant to go down this route of theorizing and deriving meaning that we don't understand from prediction in Quran and Sunnah? It is a very important theological perspective. It is necessary to understand not just judgement day but also the Quran and Sunnah overall. Our methodology is to understand the Quran and Sunnah at face value. We don't believe the Quran and Sunnah is speaking to us in riddles. We don't believe the Quran and Sunnah are symbolic. This is the standard mainstream interpretation of Islam.

Because to claim that any speaker when he says things he doesn't mean; it signifies three reasons. Number one the speaker is uninformed. He doesn't know any better. Number two, the speaker knows the truth but wants to deceive you. This is ill-intentioned.

So, either the speaker's ignorant or the speaker has an evil intention or the speaker made an honest mistake or cannot communicate properly. They don't have the grasp of the language. So, the words they're using they're not imparting the wisdom that they have in their minds.

Otherwise, if the speaker knows his material, and the speaker desires sincerity and truth, and the speaker is eloquent, then what the speaker says is what is understood by the audience.

Allah Subhana WA Ta'ala does not lie. Allah Subhana WA Ta'ala has the best of all speech. No one speaks better than Allah SWT obviously. That is the speech of Allah Subhanahu WA Ta'ala. And Allah SWT mentions the Quran as being in clear Arabic. Allah SWT says in the Quran that, "We have revealed the Quran in Arabic, so that you can understand it".

Allah SWT is saying that 'I said it in Arabic, so that you can understand. Not so that you can read in symbols. Not so that you can read in other things'.

So, to claim that what Allah says, is not intended; is to claim that the Quran is a fairytale. The Quran is fables. And this is not the claim of the Muslim. This is the claim of those who rejected Islam.

Allah AWT says in the Quran, when the Quran is recited to them, "They say these are myths of old". So, we now have some people saying, "O Adam and Hawwa these are mythological figures. And the Quran is simply narrating a fable". The point is, some Muslims, who want to preserve the Quran, they say, "so how do we reconcile?" They have a philosophy. That philosophy is that, 'Adam AS wasn't a real person. Allah SWT knows there's no such thing as Adam. But he said it to please the minds of those 7th century Arabian people. Allah SWT is communicating with that mindset. By talking about the fables that they knew'.

Now, this is problematic because the accusation is that word of Allah SWT is intentionally deceiving. The Quran doesn't say it's a fable. You see when Allah SWT wants to set up a metaphor, Allah SWT is giving you an example. When Allah SWT was to give you a metaphor, he says it. He says that, 'I'm giving you an example. This is the example'. And when Allah SWT is telling you a story from the past, then Allah SWT says these aren' fables. This is the truth.

So, when somebody comes along and says, "O Adam and Eve is a fable. It's not real". Then you are accusing Allah SWT and the Quran of lying. And the Quran of being full of fables.

Now the exact same philosophy goes for these signs of Judgment Day. Because it is the same book. And if Allah SWT and his Messenger SAW say something about the future, that is very clear about what they are saying, then the default is that it is interpreted in a literal manor. Because when we open this door, where do we stop?

If we say the Quran is symbolic, if we say the Quran is full of symbols; then what if somebody says, "Oh that means the Sharia is also symbolic". Salah is not really Salah. Hajj is not really Hajj. Soum is not really Soum.

Now does this mean that there is no eloquence in metaphorical language? Obviously, there's an element of eloquence. Sometimes, there is a metaphorical phrase. That's how we speak. We say in English, "He was caught red-handed", and caught red-handed means what he's guilty. It doesn't mean that his hand was actually red. We say that, "He had a hand in that", that means he was involved in the affair. So, obviously there's some type of metaphor.

For example, when the Prophet SAW said, "A hole of this size has been opened in the wall of Ya'juj and Ma'juj", this could be a type of simile or metaphor, that their time is closer.

Point is when it comes to the Signs of Judgment Day, we can concede maybe one phrase that might make sense to use as a metaphor. But when you have dozens of Ayahs and Hadiths describing Ya'juj and Ma'juj, describing Dajjal describing what Dajjal is going to do, this is not metaphorical. And saying that it is a big danger.

Answering People Facing Crisis of Faith

Now, a group of people who have left Islam, they say that Ya'juj and Ma'juj is a problematic issue. That if these stories make no sense, then why are you still a Muslim? They're trying to preach to other people to leave Islam. And they say, 'just like you would find stories of other faith groups problematic of this nature, and you take them as a clear sign that their faith is wrong. Why then do you not have the same bravery and courage of your own faith?'

The response is these types of question is that, what we have we have here is a far deeper issue then simply Ya'juj and Ma'juj. And that is answering the question, 'why are you a Muslim? What brings Iman to your heart?' Is it the story of Ya'juj and Ma'juj? Are you a Muslim because of the story of Ya'juj and Ma'juj? Obviously, the answer is No. We are Muslims because we have Yaqeen that Allah SWT is true, that the Quran is true, and that the Prophet SAW is true.

How do you have that Yaqeen? Now, we get to the deeper issue. We have the Yaqeen because that is the fact that, Islam answers the big questions of life, in a way that no other faith tradition does. The simplicity of the Kalama, the simplicity of La Ilaha Ill Allah, is something that no other faith tradition has. The goal of life for a Muslim is the worship of Allah Subhana wa Ta'ala. The revelation of the Quran, and the message of the Prophet SAW are the ways to achieve that goal.

The success of the single man to come in seventh century Arabia, and change the entire course of history, in a way that no human has ever done. Every single one of the big questions of life is answered by Islam. The Quran, Allah SWT, the Akhira, morality; all of this is answered by Islam.

Now, Islam is a package deal. Within this package deal, there are suprarational subjects. Subjects that are beyond the scope of rationality. Things that our mind can neither affirm nor deny. For example, resurrection of the soul, the resurrection of the body, it is not illogical. But neither is it necessarily logical. It's beyond our scope of existence. Is this something that we can logically prove from the mind? No. But is it illogical? No. It's Supra rational, beyond rationality. Because there's a realm that the mind does not operate in.

The problem of the philosophers, and the problem of these pseudo-intellectuals is that, they feel the mind can operate in any arena. And that's false. Belief in Ya'juj and Ma'juj is one of those areas.

Now, when this person, who doesn't believe in Islam, they will say, 'Why then do you believe in these fables, if they don't make any sense?' The response is, because these stories, they come in the tradition of Quran and Sunnah, and that we have Yaqeen, because of other factors. Once we have Yaqeen, then we will accept everything the tradition comes with.

Because Yaqeen is not built on these tertiary matters. And we quote Abu Bakr as-Siddiq RA, when the Quraysh came to him and said, "Do you believe your companion, when he says he went to Jerusalem and came back in one night?" Now, it's not logical for a person of that timeframe to go to Jerusalem and come back in one night. Neither is it impossible. Neither is it rational, nor is it irrational. It is definitely a miracle.

And Ibn Hisham said in his Seerah, that some people of weak Iman, they were troubled by this. Now, Abu Bakr As-Siddiq RA said, "If he said it, is true". Abu Bakr As-Siddiq RA said that because his Iman in the Prophet SAW was not based upon Isra and Miraj. It was based upon Yaqeen in Prophet SAW. He knew the sincerity of Prophet SAW.

So if your heart is at peace; and you have Iman and Yaqeen going together deep to the core, and once we know Islam to be true, and then if we come across a story that is perhaps incomprehensible, we will have to deal with it with Iman in our hearts. If you don't have Iman in your heart, which is basically the main problem for these murtads. Then obviously everything of this nature will only increase your doubt. And there is nothing that can be done about them.

Era of Peace

Now, after Ya'juj and Ma'juj, there shall be a period of luxury and peace the likes of which this world has never seen since the beginning of time. Our Prophet SAW mentioned that, one pomegranate will suffice an entire tribe and one shank of lamb will be eaten by an entire subdivision of a city. In other words, the earth will give like never before.

In one version it says that, the snakes will play with the toddlers, and the wolves will play with the Lambs.

What we see in this is that, after all of that fighting for years and years, fighting Dajjal, and then escaping Ya'juj and Ma'juj; those that live through, Allah SWT will give them some peace. This is the Sunnah of Allah SWT.

Those people that saw the worst of the worst; and we do not want to be amongst them. We should seek refuge in Allah SWT from living to see Dajjal. But if those people that are there and they manage to go through those years of turmoil and trial; that generation, then they shall be blessed like no other generation has been blessed, since the beginning of time.

How long will this time frame be? Some hadiths mention seven years. And this is proven by our Prophet SAW saying, "Wallaahi, you shall be performing Hajj and Umrah to the Kaaba even after Ya'juj and Ma'juj". That's pointing to these seven years. Now, the fact that he says "you'll be **performing** Hajj", means it is more than one Hajj.

For a few years, there shall be peace in this world. There will be no fighting. No two people will fight one another. Can you believe it? That has never happened since Habil and Qabil. But Allah SWT will bless those people. When they have seen how evil war is, for those years, no two people will ever have an argument. There will be utter peace on this earth.

Now, unfortunately with that peace and stability, some people's hearts or maybe the next generation that is born; their hearts will become hard and lack Iman. But these years will be the best years of all of mankind. But we don't want to live to see them. Because we have to go through something to see them.

Death of Isa AS

Eventually, Isa AS will die and the Mahdi will die. We don't know when. Now, Isa AS according to some narrations, will died a natural death and will be buried in the Hijr of the Prophet SAW in Medina. Now, this is not an authentic hadith. But there are such hadiths.

Of them, is the hadith of Abdullah Ibn Amr Ibn Al-As, which is not authentic. That the Prophet SAW is reported to have said, "Isa will come down to this earth. He will get married. And children will be born to him. And he will live for forty-five years". He was taken up at the age of 33. So, he will live till he's 45. So, another 13 years.

Prophet SAW said, "Then he shall die and he shall be buried with me in my Kabr. Then I and Isa Ibn Maryam will stand up together. And between us will be Abu Bakr and Umar". Now, this hadith is reported in a number of very obscure books. All of Ulema say that this hadith is very weak.

There is a narration ins Sunnah Tirmidhi, but it's not a hadith. Abdullah ibn Salam, who is the ex-Rabbi of Medina. He was the senior-most rabbi of Medina, when the Prophet SAW came. In Hadith number 3617, Abdullah bin Salam said, and not the Prophet SAW. He said, "It is written in the Torah, the description of the

Prophet SAW. And it is written in the Torah the description of Isa ibn Maryam. And the two of them will be buried together".

Who said this? Abdullah ibn Salam. It is not a hadith. He is getting this prediction from his version of the Torah. Which is clearly not around in our times. Because Jewish Arabs of that time they have a different tradition altogether. They are not connected to the mainstream Jewish Diaspora that was alive at the time. So, their beliefs and their books are slightly different. And that is very interesting, because then we get a window into a preserved Judaism that didn't exist in Babylon or in Jerusalem.

But apparently Abdullah bin Salam had some books handed down generation to generation. That the rest of Jewish folklore doesn't have any more. And in it **he** is saying, that ISA AS and Prophet Muhammad SAW are going to be buried together.

One of the narrators of this hadith, the third narrator in the chain, he said, "There is still a space in the Hijr of the Prophet SAW that can accommodate Isa Ibn Maryam AS".

Now, that is a fact that in the Hijr of Prophet SAW, there is still space for one more body over there. That much is a fact. Whether it will be Isa AS or not, Allah SWT knows best. The Narration is not authentic. But Abdullah bin

Salam was very acknowledged chief rabbi. So, Allah SWT knows best. Perhaps, Isa AS will die a natural death and perhaps he will be buried in Medina, or perhaps that is not going to happen.

Wind from Yemen

Now, what's going to happen with the followers of Isa AS, the righteous Muslims? This is where the actual end of times begins. And it will begin with a very peaceful ending. What is that peaceful ending?

Sahih Muslim reports from Abu Hurairah RA that the Prophet SAW said, "Allah SWT will send a wind from Yemen that is softer than silk. That shall not leave anyone that has an ounce of Iman in his heart, except that he shall pass away a peaceful death".

The hadith is in Sahih Muslim. So, a wind will come from Yemen, with beautiful fragrance. It will be sweet. It will be gentler than silk. When the people smell it, if they have Iman, they will die a peaceful and natural death. If they don't have Iman, they're still going to be there. And they will not die.

Jahiliya at the End of Times

Now, what do you think is going to happen, when in the whole earth, nobody of Iman is left? This is what our Prophet SAW said, "That after this point in time, idolatry will return to the Arabs". And by Arabs, he meant the children of the Muslims.

And he said that, "The women, their bodies will be doing Tawaf around the tribes of the ancient". And he said, "The people will become worse than animals. They will copulate in public like donkeys". Now this hadith is mentioned as pre-Qiyamah, and as also near end of Qiyamah. So, Allah SWT knows best.

It appears that, there will be a time where Fahisha shall be prevalent even before the Mahdi. And then there will be a time that will become even more prevalent before the actual trumpet is going to be blown.

Quran Will be Taken Back

Now, if there are no Muslims, what will happen to the Kalama? What will happen to the Salah? What will happen to the Quran? Abdullah Ibn Masud RA said, "A night will come, that the entire Quran will be taken back by Allah Subhana WA Ta'ala. The people will wake up and the Mushafs will be blank. And there will be no one with the Quran in their hearts". This is a report in Musnad al-Darimi.

In another version, he said to his students, "Make sure you read the Quran before it is taken away". The students said, "O teacher, these Mushafs, how can they be taken away?" And Ibn Masud RA said, "A night will come, when the Quran will be taken away and nobody will remain who can recite a single verse. And they will even forget La Ilaha Ill Allah. And they will speak the speech of Jahiliyyah". It means, they're going to talk the Fahisha, vulgarity, evil stuff.

Now, this is when Allah SWT's statement that is Surah An-Naml verse number 82, is going to happen. what is this statement? it talks about the beast.

In another version, Ibn Masud RA said that, "The Quran will be taken away in one night and not a single verse will be left in the Kalb of any servant. And not a single

Mushaf will remain with the speech on it. And the people will wake up like animals.

Now, it is pretty obvious therefore, that the previous hadith and this hadith go together. That the day that, that wind blows, is the day the Quran will be gone. And even those had memorized some Surah and verses, but they weren't Mumin, they will wake up the next day and they will remember nothing. And the physical printed Mushafs, they will become empty. Nothing will be there.

What will happen to the Kalama? In Sahih Muslim, Anas Ibn Malik RA said that, the Prophet SAW said that, "Qiyamah will not take place until no one says on this earth, Allah, Allah". Think about that. Qiyamah will not take place until nobody says Allah. Anyone who says is gone. When will that happen? Obviously after the wind comes.

Hudhayfah ibn al-Yaman RA said, "Islam will be wiped away. Just like a garment that is continually worn, is worn out. Until no one will know what is Siyam, and what is Salah, and what is Hajj, and what is Sadaqa".

Subhan Allah! Salah will be gone. Sadaqa will be gone. Hajj will be gone. Everything will be gone. Islam will be wiped away. Until no one knows what anything is. And in one night, the Book of Allah Subhanahu WA Ta'ala will be wiped away as well. Until not a single Ayah remains.

Now this is very interesting, because this is Hudhayfah ibn al-Yaman RA saying it from the Prophet SAW, and Ibn Masud RA also said it from himself. The to put together, clearly shows this is an authentic article.

So, Hudhayfah ibn al-Yaman RA says, "A night will come where the whole Quran will be taken away; and there shall be remaining a small group of people. An elderly man and an elderly lady, very old people, and they will reminisce. And they will say, 'We remember our forefathers saying La Ilaha Illa Allah. But we don't know what it means. So, we also will just say it like they said it'".

So, Silla Ibn Zufar RA, the student of Hudhayfah ibn al-Yaman RA said, "O Hudhayfah ibn al-Yaman RA, of what use will it be, that they say la Ilaha Illa Allah and they don't know what it means? And they're not praying, and they're not fasting, and they're not giving charity, and they're not going for Hajj?"

Now, this hadith is pointing at a very deep theological subject, that is not related to the signs of Judgment Day. But it is very interesting, because this hadith is one of the evidences used for, what does it mean to be a Muslim. Is it enough to say you're a Muslim, and not do anything?

There are so many people, our own children and grandchildren in the Muslim communities whose parents are Masha 'Allah the best of the best. And their sons and daughters have nothing to do with this religion whatsoever. Other than the title.

It's very common. Are they Muslim? Some Ulema said, "no". Some Ulema said, "Yes". And those that said, "Yes have a long list of evidences. And they primarily used this hadith.

Now, the Muslims who were brought to America as slaves, they were not able to preserve their religion. They were not able to preserve their Islam completely. Allah SWT knows how many Muslims came. But they are in the tens of thousands in the very least. Think about that. Muslims were brought here from West Africa and from the coasts of Africa.

They were brought here as slaves. We know so many of them, like Ayub ibn sulayman. We know them. We have pictures of them. We have handwritten documents in the Smithsonian. We still have Qurans that they wrote from memory. We still have them in this land. These were slaves that had memorized the Quran. Some of them were Ulema. Some of them were princes.

Now, there was this slave owner back in the 1800s, who came across a Muslim slave and appreciated the Islam of that slave. And he realized that Muslims are educated. Muslims can manage finances. And Muslims are trustworthy. So, he made it a point to purchase Muslim slaves. And he had a plantation off the coast of Georgia, on an island called Sapelo Island.

So, on the Sapelo Island, there was a large concentration of Muslim slaves. And they would establish the Salah, they had a Masjid. That is actually the first Masjid of America. They celebrated Eid.

How do we know this? Because the owners and the descendants of the owners kept Diaries and they talked about these Muslim slaves. They mentioned that there was a festival, in which they baked a particular cake. That we now know it was the cake that Muslims would make on Eid-ul-Fitr. Obviously, then slavery is abolished. Everything changes. Sapelo Islands remains disconnected from the mainland.

In the 1930s Harvard University sent a group of anthropologists to study the descendants of slaves. And they have a very extensive archive of audio and video material. Because they wanted to preserve the accents. They wanted to preserve the heritage. Not just in Sapelo, but across America. It was a very well researched project.

They went to the Sapelo island. And they interviewed the grandchildren of those people. They interviewed people in their 80s and 90s, who have memories of their ancestors three to four generations ago. And what you read is mind-boggling.

One of these people says, "I remember I had an uncle Us kids would always make fun of him. Because he would go to one of the corner trees, and fall flat on his face a few times a day".

And another lady says, "I had an aunt that she would always say phrases that would make us children laugh". And she said, "I don't remember them exactly. but it's something like 'Ash Mada Gatta'". So, the aunt used to say "Ash Hadu An La Ilaha Illallah". But this is what the decedent remembers now.

Similarly, A lady, she remembers one of her ancestors. She said, "My aunt Henrietta would always have something on her head. And she would always say these phrases that would make us kids laugh". This is a lady is ninety years old, at the time of the interview. Then she says that, "And she had a phrase that she used to say". Then she gives phase that sound like Ayahs of Quran.

Of course, these children are no longer Muslim. There Islam is all gone obviously. But this hadith reminds us of that. That Islam is gone, but some phrase remains. So, it's not just towards the end of times.

Now, in Andalus, there was a person who converted back to Islam in the 80s. He was scared that his Catholic family, and especially his grandmother, who was a very hardcore Catholic, would get angry at him if she found out. So, he would lock the door when he prayed, when he visited his grandmother. One day he thought he locked the door, but he didn't and his grandmother opened the door. He was in Sajda and he panicked.

His grandmother sat down next to him and began to cry. The man became flustered. He said the Salaam. And then he consoled his grandmother. He told her not worry. That everything is fine and normal.

The grandmother said, "No. I'm not crying because you converted to Islam. I'm crying because my grandmother told me that we are of those Muslim families. And She told me to preserve Islam. At least in knowledge that we are Muslim. And I didn't do that. And seeing you prostrate obviously put all of these emotions back into me".

Now the question is, are you a Muslim if you don't do anything? The general rule is that if you're living in a land of Islam, or in a land where Islam can be practiced, and you refuse to lower your head in Sajda even once, and you refuse to fast even once, and you refuse to do anything of Islam, then mere self-identification does not make you a Muslim.

However, in exceptional circumstances, like the Sapelo Islands, like Andalus; in those circumstances may be there is an excuse. That excuses only applies when you don't have access to other Muslims. When you're all alone. When you're persecuted. in that case, if you don't do anything other than say I'm a Muslim, perhaps that will be enough for you. This is proven in this Hadith.

Now, coming back to the hadith, Hudhayfah ibn al-Yaman RA said, "O my student Silla, it will save them from the fire of hell. That Kalama will save them from Jahannam".

So, when there's nothing left, perhaps identifying with Islam is all that is needed. But this is an exceptional situation and Scenario. Now what this also shows, as an elderly man will say "I remember my forefathers say La Ilaha Illa Allah", means there shall be an entire generation that is raised after the wind of Yemen.

There will be at least 40 to 60 years and in that new generation that comes, may be simply knowing there's something called Islam, and wanting to be it, could be their excuse. But the default will be that these people will be the worst of the worst. They will be animals or worse than animals.

Because, there is no Salah, there is no Quran, there is no Kalama, there is no morality. They will live like animals. And upon this generation the actual trumpet will be blown.

Interpretation of Surah Al-Isra

Now, we will incorporate a very interesting explanation of the beginning of Surah Al-Isra. Because this is now another interpretation of a very classical set of verses that many Ulema of our times are interpreting as being one of the signs of Judgment Day.

The Surah starts off with the subject of Isra and the fact that Allah Subhana WA Ta'ala blessed the Bani Israel and that he gave them some power in the land. And the verses then go on. This is verse number 4 of Surah Al-Isra. These are very powerful verses. Allah SWT says, "We conveyed and decreed to the children of Israel in the kitab". What is the Kitab here? Most of our Ulema say that it is Al Lawh Al Mahfooz.

So, Allah SWT says, "We decreed amongst Al Lawh Al Mahfooz, to the Bani Israel, that you shall cause facade in this world twice. And you shall reach a degree of great haughtiness". Interestingly enough, Allah SWT uses the same adjective for Firon in the Quran as well.

Meaning is that, Allah SWT is saying that the Bani Israel will have two periods of might and Izzah, that they will abuse. Allah SWT says, "When the first of these two promises come, when the first time comes that you shall rise up, you shall be dominant; when that time comes you shall cause façade".

What is façade? Facade is corruption. Facade is killing. Facade is subjugation of people. Facade is lots of chaos wherever they are. Facade is caused by corrupt people, by evil people.

So, Allah SWT is saying that when the first of these two times Bani Israel is going to make the façade happen, "A group will come against you. They are our creation. Our servants. We created them. They have great military might. They are strong nation. And they will manage to go and probe even into your houses. And this was a promise that indeed took place. It is a true promise".

And Allah SWT says, "Then we gave you back a new chance and we caused you to have a victory over your enemies. So, from being subjugated, being humiliated, you rose up again from the ashes and you developed power. And we gave you blessings. You now have a civilization, children, wealth. And we made you powerful in numbers. Ya Bani Israel, if you do good, it's only for yourself. But if you do evil, it will be used against you".

Then, Allah SWT is saying, "If you are faithful to your commandments, if you obey Allah, you will benefit yourself. Your nation will thrive. You will become more powerful. But if you misuse that power, and if you subjugate others and cause tyranny and façade, then that will be taken away from you, when the second and final time power comes. Because there shall not be a third time of power".

So, as per Quran, "Ya Bani Israel, Allah has decreed that you shall come to power and be a civilization twice. the first one is already decided. The second one, when it shall happen, Allah will send another group of people and they will cause your faces to become sour. Because when you're hurt, when you're irritated, when you're angry, your faces scowl. After they were beaming with pride, they will now become scowling with anger. And they shall enter the Masjid Al-Aqsa, as they entered it the previous time. And they will destroy whatever you had taken over. whatever you had built, all of it will be destroyed and taken away".

And then Allah Subhana WA Ta'ala says, "Your Lord might have mercy on you. And if you go back to your evil ways, we will go back to our punishing of you. And we have made Jahannam a place for the Kuffar to reside in".

Now, what is the Tafseer of these Ayahs of Surah Al-Isra? Most of the early commentators from early Islam, they said that these two highs for the Bani Israel have already taken place. They are in the past. They have said that, the first of these was the Assyrian exile of 722 BC. Meaning, pointing to the time when the Assyrians attacked the remnants of the original Kingdom of Israel that was founded by Dawood AS and Suleman AS.

Kingdom of Dawood AS and Suleman AS after their passing was on splintered into two. And then one these two disintegrated. One of them remained. One that remained was finally gotten rid of by the Assyrians who attacked them in 722 BC. And then another group came and eventually the Babylonian expulsion took place under Nebuchadnezzar in 597 BC. So, this is one interpretation that the first high of pawer for Bani Israel was 722 BC and the second of them was 597 BC.

Others have said, and this was very popular interpretation as well. This is the position of even some of the Tabi'un. That the first of these highs is 597 BC, when the second temple was destroyed. So, there were two temples. The original Temple of Solomon that Allah Azza Wajal blessed Suleman AS with. That the Jinns helped him to build a magnificent structure that people could marvel at. Because it wasn't built by humans only.

This was the Jinn that helped Suleiman AS built the most magnificent icon in the whole world at that time and this was destroyed in 722 by the Assyrian invasion. And then they built a second temple. And the King Herod built the other temple which was then destroyed under the Roman destruction of 70 CE. This is after Jesus Christ AS.

So, from 722 BC, there was no temple. Then King Herod built the temple again. And it was there for a few decades. Then in 70 BC, the Romans came and destroyed the temple. And the Wailing Wall that we see today is the only remnants of the second temple built by King Herod. As for the Temple of Solomon, nothing remains of it. What we have is the second temple's one wall remaining, and that's the western wall, or the Wailing Wall; that was built around the time of Jesus AS. That is now the wall that they go and they worship at.

So, as per Tabi'un the first high of power is the expulsion of Nebuchadnezzar because Nebuchadnezzar massacred them. It was one of the main massacres of the Bani Israel. He almost exterminated Bani Israel, that they had to flee to various places in the world. And then in the Roman expulsion that took place in 70 CE was the end of the other wave of political high. This is the classical interpretation that the two have already occurred.

Now, there is a modern interpretation that a number of prominent Ulema from across the globe have agreed upon. A number of prominent Scholars in Egypt, in Balad As-Sham, and Palestine, and number of places, they are saying that, 'Why are we assuming that both of these are in the past? The Quran doesn't say so. In fact, the Quran only says the first one has taken place. As for the second, the Quran does not say that it has taken place. Why are we assuming it has taken place?'

So, the first one would then most likely be the first destruction of the temple that was when the glory of the original Kingdom was completely gone. And they have never had that type of political stability up until today. So, with the creation of modern state of Israel, the second high begins.

So, the interpretation is that, Allah SWT is saying that, 'We give you one more chance and you were victorious over your enemies. We helped you. We aided you. You had government aid. You had the largest endowments from the biggest superpower in the world. You had everything you could have ever wanted. You couldn't have asked for more. With all of this what did you do? If you acted properly that would have been for your own good'.

"So then when the second time comes, **another group will come,** and this group will eliminate the Izzah that you had. And you shall see that your facade and your evil did not help you. And you will see it. And your faces will demonstrate that".

Now here's the key point, that allows them to make this Tafseer. The **group** that is being referenced here it is not alien to **Masjid Al-Aqsa.** This group has already conquered Masjid Al-Aqsa at some previous point in history. And now they are conquering it again.

Who conquered Jerusalem once before and wants to conquer it again? The Ummah. And Umar ibn Al-Khattab RA is the one who conquered it the first time. So, this is another interpretation and it is gaining more and more traction. And frankly this phrase of "Another group will come that had Al Aqsa before" is very powerful.

And it's a very, very, plausible tafseer. And this will give us hope. And we already talked about the Mahdi. So, all of this, could be a part of that time.

Now, this isn't the only interpretation. There are a number of other interpretations here as well. And we'll just mention two other interpretations. The first of them, says that, the Kitab here is the Al Lawh Al Mahfooz. And in this opinion, the first rule is not of the past either. Rather, in this opinion, the first one is happening right now.

And the reasoning is the phrase, "Ibadal Lana"; that this opinion applies to Muslims. So, it means Muslims will take over this land. The context seems to indicate that. Therefore, this must be the Muslim Ummah. And we shall see this, maybe soon in our lifetime. That Muslims might get Al Aqsa back. Then there will be a reconquest under the time of the Madi and the Isa AS.

Another opinion, that interprets these Ayahs in a completely unique and unprecedented manner. It says that the Ayahs are talking to Muslims and not Bani Israel.

In this interpretation Allah SWT is saying, "Then we gave back to you, o Muslims, and not the Bani Israel, the victory and we in reinforced you all Muslims with wealth and Sons. And we made you O Muslims more numerous and powerful. Then when the final promise comes, meaning now with the rise of a modern political entity and a modern country, now when this entity comes, they will sadden your faces, O Muslims".

This opinion swapped it around completely. Given the word used in the Ayah is My slave, that can apply to anyone. Muslims and non-Muslims alike.

So, rather than saddening the faces of Bani Israel, Allah SWT is telling us, "o Muslims, you shall be humiliated by them. They had the Masjid once upon a time. They will have it one more time". So, situation is completely flipped.

Then next Verse is saying, "And they will destroy the region, the farms and the people. Impose a blockade. You will be in the largest open-air prison in the world. O Muslims, perhaps your Lord will have mercy. Be patient". Because as Ibn Abbas RA said, "Every time Allah SWT says in the Quran word 'Assa', it will happen".

So, it means, "Your Lord shall have mercy on you. o Muslims, who are being persecuted; o Muslims who are dying; o Muslims who are becoming Shaheed; being jailed; don't worry Allah will have mercy on you. When you return to your Deen, Allah will honor the promise to protect you". Things are completely flipped over in this interpretation.

"When you O Muslims are faithful to the religion, Allah will be faithful to his promise". So, this is a promise from Allah SWT that, "they shall rise again and they shall humiliate you". But Allah SWT is saying, "Don't worry. The minute and the day you stand up to your principles, we shall return to ours". So, this is a very interesting interpretation.

Three Zalazil

Now, as it was said earlier that there is no particular order to the ten major signs. We have covered Dajja and Ya'juj and Ma'juj. We now move on to the other final signs. Of them, is the three earthquakes. For the three earthquakes, there is nothing that has been mentioned about them, other than their title.

No major description and details are there. Nothing else is mentioned. Except in one hadith. That says, "One will be in the east, and one will be in the West, and one will be in Jazirat al-Arab". So, one will be on one side of the world. Another will be on the other side of the world. And one will be in Jazirat al-Arab.

What we can infer though, is that these earthquakes will be on an unprecedented scale. Something that mankind has never seen. Why? Because the very fact that they deserved the mention in **Major** signs, in a category where Dajjal and Ya'juj and Ma'juj are mentioned; it means these earthquakes will be as catastrophic to mankind, as Dajjal and Ya'juj and Ma'juj.

The mention to the level of **Major** signs indicates that they are not your typical earthquakes. This is going to be something totally beyond what mankind is used to. And that is why they are mentioned as being of these signs.

Now, an interesting hypothetical point which is made is that, it does not mention whether these earthquakes are direct acts of God, or perhaps caused by something human beings are doing on this earth. It simply says, three times the earth Zalazil will take place.

So, this goes back to a theory, and Allah knows best; that is the possibility, that all of these weaponries and all of this arsenal being used, and when all of these people let loose upon one another, might be the cause of the earthquakes.

So, either these three Zalazil are directly from Allah SWT as acts of God, or these three Zalazil are permission by Allah for humans to cause. Either way, there are going to be three massive, cataclysmic, earth-shattering, earthquakes; that will take place in three parts of the world. These are three of the ten signs of Judgment Day.

The Dukhan

Another of the signs, and again Allah SWT knows the order. As the Prophet SAW said, "These are the ten major Signs. When you see one of them, the others will come one after the other". We don't know the order of the ten signs.

One of these ten signs is the Dukhan. The Dukhan is a smoke, cloud, fog. That the skies are dark. Again, it is a plausible interpretation, that this cloud will be from all the weapons being used. And only Allah SWT knows if it's something man-made or something completely directly caused by Allah Subhana WA Ta'ala.

Allah SWT says in the Quran in Surah Dukhan, verse number 10. So, this is a sign that is mentioned in the Quran. That "Just wait, until the day comes when the skies will be full of a clear Dukhan". So, Allah SWT is saying "Just wait" as a threat. And clear Dukhan is an oxymoron. Clear Dukhan means that the Dukhan will be manifest. The Dukan will be visible.

The Quran says, "Dukhanim Mubin", it means a manifest Dukhan. The Dukhan that is blatant, everywhere. And Quran says, "It will envelope all of mankind. That will be a very difficult Azab". What is this Dukhan that will envelope the globe? May be a mushroom-shaped cloud.

What is this Dukhan that will take over this whole earth, and all of mankind will see it, and all of mankind will recognize this is a calamity and a tragedy that is unprecedented. Now we are not predicting Ilm Al Ghaib. But this makes a lot of sense, given all that is happening.

So, the point being that, there is going to be Dukhan, and this Dukhan will envelope the whole world. And this Dukhan will terrify the people. Allah SWT knows what other impact it might have on the people. And the people will recognize this is a tragedy of the highest magnitude. All of mankind is enveloped. And this is a very difficult and very painful punishment from Allah SWT.

In this dunya, there will be an Azab from this Dukhan that perhaps mankind has never seen before. Now, this is the Dua that we should memorize. May Allah protect us from ever having to use it. Because we don't want to be alive when all of this happens.

If we see the Dukhan, those who are alive when the Dukhan happens, this is a dua they can say. it is the Ayah number 12 of Surah Dukhan,

رَّبَّنَا ٱكْشِفْ عَنَّا ٱلْعَذَابَ إِنَّا مُؤْمِنُونَ

Now, Ibn Masud RA and his students, considered the Dukhan as having already occurred in a certain time in Makkah. That there was a drought and a sandstorm came. And it affected the Quraysh. And it was like a type of punishment for them. So, Ibn Masud said, that The Dukhan has taken place. And his students followed him in this.

However, the other Sahaba disagreed. And this is the dominant position. In fact, that the Ayah itself seems to indicate that the Dukhan is going to take place in the context of Judgment Day. It says, "Wait, until Judgment comes". Because this is how the Quran addresses the Quraysh.

So, the Quran and even the Sunnah mentions this issue of the Dukhan. The Sunnah does not mention anything authentic about the description of the Dukhan. It simply says, "Of the ten signs is the Dukhan, a great cloud that will appear across all of the world".

Sun rising from the West

Another sign of these ten major signs is the rising of the Sun from the West. This is not something that the Quran explicitly mentions. But there is an implied verse. Allah says in the Quran, this is Surah Al-An'am, verse number 158 that, "The day that some of the signs of your lord will come, it will not benefit anyone to accept faith at that time, if they had not accepted faith before".

Now, the Quran does not say, the Sun will rise from the West. The Quran simply says, "when some of the signs will come, Iman is of no use". Where do we learn that this Ayah is a reference to the Sun rising from the West? From hadith literature. And this is authentic. Both in Buhari and Muslim.

And in this hadith from both Sahih Buhari and Sahih Muslim, the Prophet SAW said, "Qiyamah will not occur until the Sun rises from the West. And when the people see it, they will all believe". Then the Prophet SAW recited this verse that, "when they see some of the signs of their Lord, it will not matter if they believe at that time, if they hadn't believed before".

So, our Rasool Allah SAW linked this Ayah with the Sun rising from the West. And in another hadith in Abu Dawood, the Prophet SAW said that, "The first of the signs will be the rising of the Sun from the West and

right after it at Salat Ad-Duha, the Dabbat will come"
The time for Salat Ad-Duha Baha, as our Prophet SAW
said, is after Fajr and before Zohar. At that Time the
Beast will come.

And the Prophet SAW said, "Whichever of these comes
first, the next one will follow immediately". In other
words, maybe the Dabbat will come at Ad-Duha and
then the Sun will come from the West the next day. Or
maybe the Sun will come from the West and the same
day, because that's going to be the Fajr time, the same
day the Beast will come.

So, there are at least seven hadiths, three of them at
least in Bukhari and Muslim; that mentioned the Sun
rising from the West. Now this is something that is
explicit. It is authentic.

Now some have made reinterpretation of this as well.
There have been some people that say, this Hadith
means Islam will dominate in the west. That Sun rising
from the west is a metaphor. And the metaphor is that
Islam coming from the West, shall dominate the globe.

This interpretation is not correct. Because the whole
point here is that, the Prophet SAW is saying and the
Quran is saying, "When they see this sign, Iman is of no
use". This means that this is a sign that is simply beyond
question. It will be beyond reason of a doubt. It will be
self-Evident. It's like the Magicians of Firon, when they

saw the staff become a snake, and they knew Musa AS was the Prophet of SAW. And they became Muslims right there and then.

So, this is not some metaphor, for Islam coming from the West. Because that's not something that is that amazing, that all the people will accept Islam. No. That doesn't make any sense. This clearly seems to be something that, we just have to believe is the very last day of the existence basically, that the creation will change.

Literally, it's something that will happen right before the trumpet is being blown. It's something that is actually understandable even. Everything will change before the trumpet is blown. This is the standard position of all of our Ulema. And this will essentially be, on the very last day of existence of creation. That is why, there is no point of a person accepting Islam. It's too late.

It's like Firon, when he sees the Angel of Death, he says, "Oh I see the angel of death. I believe now". And what does Allah SWT say? He says, "Now?" That a rhetorical question from Allah SWT that, "Now, you're going to accept? After all of this? No. It's not going to be accepted of you".

Our Prophet SAW said, "Allah will accept the Tawba of any person, until he sees the Angel of Death". Because the veil between this world and the other is lifted at time of death. And the person can clearly see the truth. So, when you see the angel of death, that is it. Same concept applies to sun rising from the west.

Now in another hadith, Prophet SAW says, "Allah will accept Tawba of any person until the Sun rises from the West". So clearly there is an indication that the Sun shall rise from that portion. And it will be something that is manifest and clear. This is not normal. And this is going to be the final day and everything is going to come to an end. And Allah SWT knows best.

The Dabbat

Now we get to the subject of the Dabbat. And the Dabbat or the beast is mentioned in the Quran. Dabbat is mentioned in the Quran in Surah an-Naml, Verse number 82. This is in the Quran that, "Once the command has been given", which means once judgment is given, then Khallas, it's too late. Now, once the motion has been set in, that's it. End is coming. The end is near.

The Quran says, "We shall bring out for them a beast from this earth. The Beast will speak to them. And it will say people would not believe in our Signs".

Our Prophet SAW said, hadith is in Sahih Muslim, that, "Three are the things, when they appear, there is no Fayda in a person accepting Iman, if they hadn't accepted it before this". Number one, "The rising of the Sun from the West". Number two, "the Dajjal". And number three, "The beasts of the earth".

Now, there is some Ikhtilaf between Ulema over the mention of Dajjal. But the point is that these two are explicitly mentioned; the rising of the Sun from the west and the Dabbat or the beasts of the earth. When these two happen, then there is no repentance. And if a person has not accepted Iman, it will not be accepted after this.

What is this Dabbat? What are the details? The Quran has only this one verse. In the hadith, there are a lot of apocryphal hadiths. Hadiths that are found in the very obscure works. As for the famous six books of hadith, the only authentic hadith mentions Dabbat. But without any description. It just mentions the beasts of the earth.

There is a hadith in Tirmidhi, that is a weak Hadith as well. It is not an authentic hadith. But the hadith says that, "The Dabbat shall have with it, the staff of Musa AS and the ring of Suleiman AS". However, this seems to be coming from Judeo-Christian sources. Where the Beast will have the staff and the ring.

In Musnad Imam Ahmed, there is a hadith that is weak. It is not authentic. In which it says that, the Dabbat will mark people with a symbol. The Dabbat will stamp people with Iman and Kufr. Dabbat will mark who's a Muslim and who is a kafir.

This hadith first is not authentic. Secondly, it is problematic in terms of its content. The problematic issue that this weak hadith has is, that it says, that the Dabbat will stamp people as Mumin and kafir. But when is the Dabbat coming? Literally, the last day of existence. There are no Mumin left in earth. So even from the perspective of content it doesn't make any sense.

By the time the Dabbat becomes, the Quran and the Kalama are taken away. Allah, Allah is not being mentioned on earth. We have already mentioned that before. That generation will come, where there is no actual Quran left.

now there are at least a dozen traditions that are found in the very obscure works. In some of these, there is some inexplicable understanding. That the Dabbat shall be the she-camel of Saleh AS, that will be resurrected again. Or that the Dabbat is the child of that she-camel of Saleh AS.

in any case, Allah knows best. We don't have any information about the Dabbat. So, we leave it as it is. It is a beast, that is one of the signs of the last day. That's all that we need to know.

Now all of us have heard of the beast. We know about the beast, unfortunately, not through the Quran. We know it from Christian folklore. Because it is something that is common in Christian folklore. The beast is of course believed in by many strands of Christianity. And that is because the Book of Revelations mentions the Beast.

In fact, the book of Revelation mentions two beasts. The Beast of the water, and the beast of the earth. And this is interesting because the title is the Beast of the land. And in the Quran "Dabbat Al-Ard" translate to the beast from the land. The Book of Revelations also mentions that the enigmatic number is 666 that will come with the beast. We have no such thing as 666. That's only found in Judeo-Christian literature.

And as said before, that the Sun rising from the west and the Dabbat, will occur within 24 hours of each other. And it is essentially the last of the 10 signs, before the trumpet will be blown. What it looks like from the hadith is that, when the Sun rises from the West, the Dabbat will come out in two-three hours. Because that's after Fajr time. And the trumpet will be blown on that same day later on. And Allah SWT knows best.

The Great Fire

Now, we have one of the signs left. And Although we are mentioning it in the end, it is not actually the last sign. But it helps in explaining the last days of mankind. This sign is probably after Wind blows from Yemen and Quran will be taken Back; and before the Dabbat and before the Sun rising from the West. And Allah SWT knows best. The tenth sign is the great fire.

Now the great fire is not mentioned in the Quran. But it is mentioned in numerous Hadiths. Of them, the most famous is in Sahih Muslim. That, "Qiyamah will not come until you see 10". And in this hadith, the Prophet SAW said, "And the last of them is the great fire".

So, there shall be something called the great fire. What is this great fire? Combining all of the hadiths together, it appears that the great fire is something that will begin from Yemen. To be more precise from Aden. In one hadith it says from Aden. Which is the port city of Aden in Yemen.

The great fire will force the people to flee from it and they will be forced to go Balad As-Sham. Now, what will be the fuel of this fire? What will cause this fire that will scorch the earth one mile after the other, and keep on going all the way from the tip of one side of the Arabian Peninsula all the way to the other side?

And it is well known that in this land most of it is nothing but sand. What will cause the fuel of this fire? Allah SWT knows best. It most likely could be a miraculous fire.

So, the people will be forced to flee for their lives. They will be walking, they'll be riding, they'll be running, they'll be on camels, and they will have to stop to rest. Our Prophet SAW said, hadith is in Sahih Muslim. Hudhaifa bin Usaid al-Ghifari RA says, "One day the Prophet SAW came to us, when we were sitting in a room and we were talking about the judgment". The Prophet SAW said, "Judgment will not come until you see ten signs".

Remember this is not in order. Number one, the rising of the Sun from the West. Number two, the Dukhan. Number three, the Dabbat. Number four, Ya'juj and Ma'juj. Number five, Isa Ibn Maryam AS. Number six, the Dajjal. Number seven, eight and nine, the three earthquakes, one in the east and one in the west and one in Jazeerat al Arab. And the last of them, number 10, is the Nar, that will come from Aden. And Aden is the famous city in Yemen.

The prophet SAW said, "It will gather the people and it will stop when they need to stop. And it will go when they're going to go". In other words, it is something that is truly miraculous. That it will force the people to flee. But in a manner that they can still rest awhile. Because you cannot walk from Aden, all the way to Balad As-sham, except in two-three weeks.

It's not going to be immediate. And in this course of time people will be forced to rest. When they rest, the fire will rest with them. When they wake up, they'll be forced to move again until they stop and that will continue to do this.

Now, once again, it appears that these people are simply not believers. Because other hadiths tell us that judgment will not come upon believers. Our Prophet SAW one day said in a hadith, that is authentic and it is in Musnad Imam Ahmed. He pointed to the north, which is Bilad As-Sham and he said, "In that direction, you will be gathered. In that direction is Ard Al Mahshar".

What is Ard Al Mahshar? Ard Al Mahshar is the land of Resurrection. Now does this mean, that Qiyamah will take place in Sham? Because Hashr is Judgment Day. The responses no. There are two types of Hashr. There is the final showdown, Hashr of this dunya. And then there is the Hashr of Judgment Day in the next life, after the trumpet.

The Hashr of this dunya, there is no Qiyamah. It is just a death. And that's what Prophet SAW is talking about. The Ard Al Mahshar is where all of the last remnants of mankind will be gathered. All of mankind, whoever remains will be gathered in one place. And that is why it is called Ard Al Mahshar. What will that land be? Balad As-Sham.

So, they will continue to go there until finally they are all gathered in one place. And then the final very end of mankind will take place. And that is the trumpet being blown.

Where Everything Began

Now, one of the things that have caused consternation is the fact that, there seems to be absolutely no mention of lands and regions far away from that central areas. And the reason why, this brings great consternation is because, a lot of us happen to be living in some of those lands, that are very, very, far away. And these lands seemed to have absolutely no mention whatsoever. It's is as if everything is simply gone.

After all of the events, everything is now back to where civilization began. And there is no solid explanation. Allah SWT knows best. Other than to say, the only thing that makes sense is that, there are no humans left except in that region. And that is terrifying. Even as it explains a lot about what we are reading. And Allah SWT knows best.

There is no mention of any land. Not even Africa, Egypt, China. These were names that the Arabs knew, and the Prophet SAW knew. Nothing is mentioned at all. We're talking about the last days of mankind. We're talking about Isa AS and the Mahdi and Dajjal. It's really this area only that is mentioned. That is Balad As-Sham and the Middle East overall.

It seems that, it will be the only region left. And at one level, it does make sense. Because where are the big powers? And where will things happen when they happen? At another level, we say Allah SWT knows best. But we have not found any reference or even a hint that there will be other places where things will be happening.

Everything seems to be happening in the central region. And this is the region where everything began in the first place. Ibrahim AS, Ismael AS, Nuh AS and according to some sources even Adam AS came from this region. But Allah SWT knows best.

The Trumpet

Now, we get to the very final point. Final conclusion of this dunya will be the trumpet. And this is something that is very explicit in the Quran and Sunnah. This is very explicit. What is the Soor or the Trumpet? It is literally a trumpet. It is something that you blow into and that voice amplifies to the sound of a trumpet.

And the Yahood they have the Soor as their religious symbol of calling people. That thing that you blow into, it is something that they consider to be sacred and holy. That's why, if you go and visit the house of an orthodox, you will find this as an icon of their faith. It is something that goes back to other faith traditions as well.

Now Allah SWT mentions that the blowing of the trumpet will be something that is very sudden. People will not expect it. Allah SWT says in the Quran that, "The affairs of the Judgment Day is like the twinkling of an eye, or even faster than that". And our Prophet SAW said, hadith is in Musnad Imam Ahmed that, "The trumpet will be blown. And as soon as people hear it, everyone will turn to face the direction of the sound".

So, when the trumpet will be blown, all of mankind will look to where that sound is coming from. And he said, "The first person to hears the trumpet will be a man who is busy repairing the tank that is meant to supply water to his camels. And he will fall dead. And the people will start falling dead after him".

Now, putting everything together, these must be the people that had fled the fire from Yemen. And they're already in As-Sham. There's no other way to put it all together. They're all walking towards Sham and the fire is behind them. Once they reach Sham after weeks of walking from Yemen to sham, now this is happening.

So, another Hadith seems to say that, at some level, life is almost back to normal. As normal, as a normal can be when you have just fled from a fire.

The Prophet SAW said, "The hour will not occur, except that a man has put a cloth in front of him to sell it. But he will not be able to sell it or fold it up. The transaction has been done, but the cloth will not be sold. The hour will not be established, until a man has milked his she-camel, and has taken away that milk. But he will not be able to drink it. The hour will not be established until a man is repairing a tank for his livestock and the water for his animals, and he will not be able to pour the water for his animals. The hour will not be established, until a man raises a Lucama of food to his mouth, and before the Lucama reaches his mouth, he will not be able to eat it".

This is a hadith that is very, very explicit. And it shows us that the Qiyamah and the trumpet will be sudden. Now, if you look at all of these examples, especially the first one; which is buying and selling a garment. It means life has come to some sense of normalcy. People have to buy and sell even as they're walking for many days and weeks. So, from this, we seem to infer that Qiyamah will be an absolutely sudden experience.

No one will be able to predict the trumpet being blown. And life will almost resume to semi normal. People will be eating and drinking. People will be buying and selling. People will be milking the camels. And then the trumpet will be blown. And the trumpet will cause all of mankind to die.

Will anyone be safe from this? The Quran mentions that there will be exceptions. What is this exception? This has caused a lot of Ikhtilaf. And we do not know. Because our Prophet SAW said, Hadith is in Sahih Bukhari, that, "When the Qiyamah trumpet is blown, the second one, and I come back to life, I will find Musa ahead of me holding on to the throne of Allah SWT. Now, I do not know, if he woke up before me, resurrected before me. Or is he one of those whom Allah SWT said there is an exception. And his first falling down, counted for this one".

What was Musa AS' first falling down? His first fainting was when he asked to see Allah Subhana wa Ta'ala. The Prophet SAW said, "I do not know. Is he one of those that the exception is for?" So, if the Prophet SAW does not know who the exception is for, there is no point in any of us discussing it.

But there will be some groups of people who will be exempted from dying after the Trumpet is blown. For example, The Angels in the heavens might not necessarily be affected by the trumpet. Now, we also know that the one who will blow the trumpet is Israfil AS.

Now, Israfil AS is not mentioned in the Quran. What is mentioned in the Quran is that the trumpet will be blown into. This is what is mentioned. So, someone is blowing into the trumpet. The name is not mentioned. He is implied. But he is not mentioned by name. How do we know therefore that is Israfil AS will blow the trumpet? From hadith literature.

In a famous hadith that is in Tirmidhi, the Prophet SAW said, "How can I relax, when Israfil AS has raised the trumpet to his lips. And he is looking at the Arsh direction, waiting for the command to come to blow". This hadith is authentic.

In Another Hadith, Prophet SAW said that, "Israfil AS is staring at the throne and he has not blinked for so long, that his eyes are now glazed like glass, out of fear that if he blinks, he'll miss the command". So, this is a sign in the world of the Angels, that Judgment Day is close.

Now, how many times will the trumpet be blown? Three times.

Assalam Waliakum wa Rahmatullahi wa Barakaatuhu,

Brothers and Sisters,

I hope you benefited from this book. If you'd like to read my other books, they are as follows;

1. Dua in Islam
2. Creation in Islam
3. Angels and Jinns in Islam
4. Adam The First Man
5. Guidance from Quran and Sunnah 1, 2 and 3
6. Seerah of Prophet Muhammad SAW 1
7. Jinns and Black Magic

Jazakallah Khair,

Made in the USA
Las Vegas, NV
19 March 2024

87454994R00187